VODOU VOODOO ~A·N·D~ HOODOO

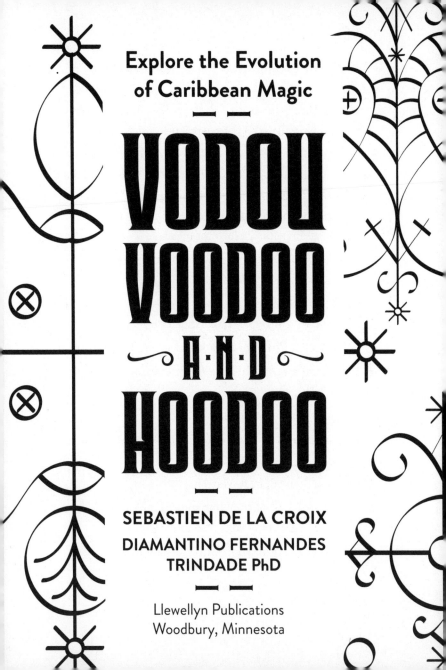

Explore the Evolution
of Caribbean Magic

VODOU
VOODOO
~A·N·D~
HOODOO

SEBASTIEN DE LA CROIX
DIAMANTINO FERNANDES
TRINDADE PhD

Llewellyn Publications
Woodbury, Minnesota

About Diamantino Fernandes Trindade

- Professor of the postgraduate course in History and Afro-Brazilian Culture at the Salesian University Center (UNISAL) between 2011 and 2015.

- Professor (retired) at the Federal Institute of Technological Education of São Paulo (IFSP), where he taught these disciplines: chemistry, foundations of education, psychology of education, history of science, and teaching epistemology.

- Received a masters in education from Universidade Cidade de São Paulo.

- Received a master of science in education science from City University Los Angeles.

- Received a PhD in education from PUC-SP.

- Received a Post-PhD in education from GEPI-PUCSP.

- Author of works on Umbanda.

- Member of the War College (Escola Superior de Guerra).

- Master Mason, Past Master.

- Vice President of the Umbandist Federation of Greater ABC between 1985 and 1989.

- Priest of the Umbanda Christian Temple of Brazil.

- Religious Minister of the House of Umbanda Culture of Brazil.
- Priest of Orunmilá-Ifá (Babáláwò Ifasoya Ifadaisi Agbole Obemo), initiated by Babáláwò Ifatoki Adekunle Aderonmu Ògúnjimi.
- Initiated in Traditional Umbanda by Father Ronaldo Linares.
- Initiated in Raiz de Guiné (Hanamatan Ramayane) by Master Yatyçara.
- Initiated in Kimbanda of the Souls (Tatá Egúngún Inú Aféfe) by Tata Kalunga.

About Sebastien de la Croix

- Initiated in Raiz de Guiné by Hanamatan Ramayane, whose disciple and spiritual son he is.
- Medium of the Umbanda Christian Temple of Brazil.
- Traditional Umbanda Priest, initiated by Father Ronaldo Linares.
- *Houngan Sur Pwen* in Haitian Vodou.
- Brazilian representative of traditional lineages of initiatory societies of the French School of Western Esotericism.
- Lawyer.

First English edition 2024
Priye Ginen courtesy of Mambo Asogwe Samantha Corfield, Bon Mambo Feraye de la Kwa Daginen (www.spellmaker.com)

Book design by Samantha Peterson
Cover design by Kevin R. Brown
Translated by Marisa Fialho Schaurich
Interior illustrations provided by the authors

Llewellyn Publications is a registered trademark of Llewellyn Worldwide Ltd.

Library of Congress Cataloging-in-Publication Data (Pending)
ISBN: 978-0-7387-7533-3

Llewellyn Publications
A Division of Llewellyn Worldwide Ltd.
2143 Wooddale Drive
Woodbury, MN 55125-2989
www.llewellyn.com

Printed in the United States of America

For the Voodoo Queen Marie Laveau.
The Queen never dies!

CONTENTS

Acknowledgments

To the Lwa who, with their powerful energy, protected us and enabled the fluidity of writing in this work.

—The Authors

To Eduardo Régis, friend and brother, also known as Frater Vameri, for his support, the fruitful conversations, and his authorization of the extensive use of his texts in this work.

Especially to my Mambo and my Houngan who, with great affection, patience, and above all, a lot of competence, unveiled the fascinating universe of Haitian Vodou to me.

—Sebastien de la Croix

FOREWORD
TO THE LLEWELLYN EDITION

Why does someone write a book? Maybe they have been told "You ought to write a book." Maybe it's ego. Maybe it's because they have something to say and want to be heard. Maybe they think it is the path to fame and fortune. There might be as many reasons as there are writers. However, in the case of *Vodou, Voodoo, and Hoodoo*, our authors had one of the most awe-inspiring reasons for writing this book for us: they felt Divinely guided. They experienced the feeling of the *Men Lespri A* (Hand of the Spirit) upon them. When this is felt, it will not be ignored. They knew they had to write this. The felt it in the depths of their spirits. Our authors answered this Call of the Spirit beautifully.

Perhaps you are wondering, now that it is written, why do I want to read it? Having read dozens and dozens of books on these subjects myself over the last fifty years, even I had to ask, "Why another one? Why do I want to read this particular book?" As I read further and further along, the answer was clear. I could feel their Divine purpose. This book has what many other books of its kind lack: heart. Heart is everything when speaking of our *Mezanmi Lwa* (Beloved Lwa). As a Mambo Asogwe of Haitian Vodou, a lifelong practitioner of New Orleans Voodoo, and having had a grandma who could whip up any Hoodoo charm you needed, I have to *feel* the heart. I have to feel at one with the authors; I have to believe they have done their best; I have to clearly see their Divine intention—these are the factors that make me believe in a book. This is what makes me believe our authors cared about the call they received to write this book. They have reverence without preaching, humor without blasphemy, knowledge without artifice. That is why I read it. That is why you should read it.

The reader should bear in mind, however, this is not meant to be an exhaustive treatise on the subject matter. Rather, it is written in concise terms, so everyone from seasoned practitioners to the mildly curious can understand and appreciate the clarity of thought presented. Most of the information we are learning in these modern times comes from what used to be strictly an oral history. For many, many years, nothing was written down. At first that was because most of the followers couldn't read and write. Later on, as that began to change, followers felt it wasn't a good idea to write these things down anyway. At one point in time, it was considered dangerous to put this information in writing lest it fall into the wrong hands and be used against you.

Of course, today we are privileged to learn from honest books like this one. It is written without the drama and sinister warnings seen all too often in writings of this kind. I encourage you to use this book—wear it out! It should be dog-eared and have your notes written in the margins. It will safely guide you and offer you a taste of the possibilities. Where you take it from here will be left up to you. Our authors have written most lovingly, caring for you with consideration of how it might affect your future path. The writing is serious, but has a bit of fun to it; it educates without unending verbosity. Our authors may help you find a spiritual path you didn't know you were looking for.

This book allows for your own thoughts and feelings. You may have read differing opinions on these subjects elsewhere. Those opinions may have been presented as facts. The differences don't really matter. The information here is sound, but flexible. The authors know very well in these traditions there are *anpil dwèt nan menm men* (many fingers of the same hand).

When I was on a trip to Haiti about twenty-five years ago, I was privileged to speak with a *Houngan* of some renown. He spoke some English; I spoke some Kreyol. Between the two of us we managed to have an amazing conversation about *anpil dwèt nan menm men*. He had noticed in his lifetime how even people of the same House did some things a bit differently. Sacred songs to the Lwa were sung differently sometimes. Vèvè, the sacred drawings used to call and honor *Les Lwa*, were sometimes drawn a bit differently. All of these differences, however, were well recognized as parts of the accepted norms; thus, there are many fingers of the same hand.

Please do not fret about minor differences of things you have read elsewhere. Instead, incorporate them. All too often, especially in America, there has been a tendency in about the last thirty years toward rigidity and rules in spiritual practices. This has choked out the idea of one's individual spiritual path and turned it into something people have learned to fear. The fear keeps people from trying and the tiny light of a spiritual path is snuffed out. Our authors would never want to see that happen to you. Yes, they are aware there are some concepts to which we must adhere. We must approach our spiritual practices in respect, with a good heart and good intentions. Our authors invite you to think and decide how (or if) you might serve and practice. It is one of the finest things about the book. It is a guide in the truest sense of the word. You are allowed to make it your own and find a spiritual path or to just find it an interesting read. No burdens are put on the reader to do or believe anything.

Being from New Orleans, I was so pleased to see accurate information presented herein. It is as accurate as it can be. New Orleans is a city of broad-brushed story-tellers, the grand raconteurs of the South. Information about colorful historical figures can be wildly dramatic and overstated. New Orleans will give the people what they want. When people come to New Orleans, they want to be thrilled and entertained about things they have seen on TV or in movies. Most every tour guide will gladly oblige, sometimes to the detriment of the real story. My relief was great to see figures like our beloved Marie Laveau presented in an engaging and intelligent way while still preserving that flare we have come to know and love. Finesse is everything in telling her story and the story of the other wonderful historical figures. Our authors most obligingly offer us just that.

There is a Haitian proverb: "*Sèl pa janm vante tèt li di l sale.*" This translates loosely as "salt does not boast that it is salty." It means you should not boast of your own accomplishments. I've always thought it dovetailed nicely with Proverbs 27:2, "Let someone else praise you, not your own mouth—a stranger, not your own lips."

As our authors would never boast about themselves, please accept from me, a stranger, my praise of them to you. They've done a good thing. Enjoy it.

—Mambo Samantha Corfield
Bon Mambo Feraye de la Kwa Daginen

FOREWORD
TO THE ORIGINAL EDITION

The most demanding reader will ask about the relevance of a book of this nature. This same reader should, however, question what impressions we commonly hear when talking about Vodou/Voodoo. It is not uncommon to come across information that is far from the reality of this rich and curious tradition. Thus, in this book, the reader has an opportunity to clarify distorted views and any frivolous impressions.

Now, the first step for a sincere seeker of spiritual traditions is not to take as truth superficial concepts given by common sense—often shaped by the culture in which one is inserted—that repeatedly introject categories and thought patterns, preventing a more flexible approach to spiritual traditions. Examples of this are the hasty misjudgments we encounter when discussing Vodou/Voodoo.

Thus, those who propose to analyze and investigate a tradition that differs from the environment in which they live must perform an inner catharsis so that their observation reaches deeper and more accurate levels.

Diamantino Fernandes Trindade and Sebastien de la Croix are profoundly serious and active researchers of various spiritual traditions, performing the services of preservation and perpetuation to bring knowledge to people and to raise interest in traditional paths of spirituality. In this work, the authors provoke the reader to deepen their understanding and learn the mysteries of Vodou/Voodoo, presenting the structure of Haitian and American worship as well as the historical, magical, and religious aspects centered on the enigmatic and eccentric figure of Marie Laveau (the Voodoo Queen), who is sometimes seen as a witch and sometimes honored as a saint.

Indeed, those who are interested in spirituality will be enchanted by the identity and characteristics of Vodou/Voodoo. Like the Brazilian religious traditions that originated on Tupiniquim soil, this tradition is the result of repression and presents a magical religious bias as well as a strong connection to Catholicism.

For those not content only with theory, in this book, there is also a space reserved for Hoodoo, a form of folk magic that contains elements of Haitian Vodou, American

Voodoo, indigenous knowledge, and European occultism. These are teachings independent of initiatory ceremonies and can be applied to other traditions. At the end of the book, we are presented with several Hoodoo recipes that contain simple practices with easily found elements.

This book will be even more pleasant if the reader allows themself to feel and assimilate Voodoo's peculiar nature and the figure of Marie Laveau, where art and magic are mixed, bringing us a harmonious combination. To that effect, the jazz and blues music of New Orleans can be excellent companions while reading, or in later moments when reflecting on the teachings that will be found here.

—Pedro Limongi (Leratsára)
Philosopher and postgraduate in Philosophy of Religion; disciple of Hanamatan Ramayane; medium of the Umbanda Christian Temple of Brazil; head of the Branch No. 1 of the Umbanda Christian Temple of Brazil (Choupana de Pai Congo)

PREFACE

Dear readers: partnered with Arole Cultural in Brazil, we present a unique work on religion and tradition, now translated and published in English by Llewellyn Worldwide. In this book, we intend to cover the incredible spiritual work of Marie Laveau and Louisiana Voodoo,[1] as well as its origins in Haitian Vodou. In addition, we will also talk about Hoodoo, a form of African American folk magic that has a lot in common with Voodoo.

We begin with a brief historical record of Haiti. Next, we approach the theology of Vodou, Haitian Vodou, and the *Ghede* (entities similar to the spirits Eshu and Pombagira, as we know them in Brazilian Kimbanda). Soon

---

1. The Voodoo Queens occupy, even today, a prominent place in the religious scene of New Orleans. Thus, we will also discuss Queen Malvina Latour, Queen Lala, Queen Marie Saloppé, and Queen Sanité Dédé in addition to Queen Marie Laveau.

after, we have the *Priye Ginen*, a long-famous Haitian recitation used in the openings of rituals, learned by heart, which greets all the African nations that participated in the formation of Vodou.

In chapter 3, we cover the two categories of Vodou spirits (Rada and Petro), spiritual beings called angels, ancestors, spirits, Mysteries, and Lwas. These beings transmit God's will and governance and link communication between people and the Divine.

Do zombies exist? That is what we will explore next. When Vodou comes up, one of the first images that comes to people's minds is that of a magically reanimated corpse to be used in manual labor on Haitian plantations. We will uncover the truth behind this mystery in the same way that we will demystify the famous and "terrible" Voodoo doll.

From Haiti, we head to New Orleans, Louisiana, and the spelling changes from *Vodou* to *Voodoo*. New Orleans oozes Voodoo, as we will see throughout this book. In this mysterious city, the fusion of French culture and Vodou took place, and many Voodoo spirits became associated with the Catholic saints who presided over the same domain. Enslaved people who were taken to Louisiana syncretized the Lwa and the saints, and although Voodoo and Catholicism are radically different, early Voodoo followers in the United States adopted the images of the

Catholic saints for their spirits as well. After all, both the saints and spirits act as mediators, such as the Virgin Mary and Legba, presiding over specific activities.

Then, in chapter 5, we finally discuss Voodoo Queen Marie Laveau, who has fascinated New Orleans with her efficient Voodoo and Hoodoo practices for several decades. She was considered one of the most powerful women in Louisiana, maintaining excellent social and political relations with priests, judges, high-ranking military officers, and other officials who sought her services. This chapter discusses aspects of both her life and her work. Marie Laveau built upon the existing doctrines of Voodoo and made it into something everyone could practice, and her reputation has been kept alive in songs, films, and novels. She was portrayed in *American Horror Story: Coven*, and in Marvel comic books in the 1970s, she was an opponent of both Dracula and Dr. Strange.

During the nineteenth century, Voodoo Queens became central figures of this religion in the United States, presiding over ceremonial meetings and ritual dances. They also earned income by administering charms, amulets, and magical powders guaranteed to heal diseases, grant wishes, and confuse or destroy enemies. Therefore, we will proceed with a section on Malvina Latour, who succeeded Marie Laveau as the Queen of Voodoo, even though Marie Laveau II remained the most remarkable figure of New

Orleans Voodoo after her mother's death. We will also discuss Laura Hunter, a famous Voodoo Queen in New Orleans from the 1930s and 1940s known as Princess Lala. (In the late 1970s, Irma Thomas, a singer from New Orleans, recorded a song called "Princess La La" based on Laura Hunter, with lyrics that tell a story.) Then, we talk about Dr. John Montanee, a Voodoo icon and one of Marie Laveau's mentors, with text based on the research of Denise Alvarado.

Finally, in chapter 7, we explore Hoodoo, a form of African American folk magic that is the union of three traditional strands of magic, healing, and folklore: Haitian Vodou, the herbal and healing knowledge of Native Americans, and the magical techniques and wisdom compiled from European texts such as the *Grimorium Verum*, *The Grimoire of Pope Honorius*, *The Book of Abramelin*, and even the *Key of Solomon*.

Soon after, we have sensational Hoodoo recipes that teach you, amongst other things, to make your own gris-gris, a traditional talisman in Hoodoo and Louisiana Voodoo. We close with Hoodoo's powerful usage of the Psalms and a traditional Hoodoo prayer to open paths. (Once again, observe the use of the spelling *Vodou* when referring to the Haitian practice and *Voodoo* in reference to the practice in the United States.)

We hope this work serves as a point of reflection for thinking brains and sensitive hearts to take a new look, free of prejudice, at the marvelous religion of Vodou/Voodoo. We wish you all a delightful read!

Somos o que somos!

A BRIEF AND NECESSARY INTRODUCTION

This small book was born in a very unpretentious way, and we decided to leave it like this: simple, short, colloquial, presenting what is necessary for the public to understand what Haitian Vodou is, its derivation to North American Voodoo, and the influence of both in the Hoodoo tradition. We hope that this book will bring some understanding of these religions and traditions and that it will undo some of the immense prejudice that still exists regarding these subjects.

The chapters referring to Vodou, Voodoo, and Hoodoo came from a small booklet prepared by Sebastien de la Croix and delivered to the participants of a workshop sponsored by the Brazilian House of Umbanda Culture in which, in addition to the theoretical teachings of these three traditions, practical Hoodoo workshops were conducted.

At the same time, extensive research on the Voodoo of New Orleans and the fascinating Marie Laveau was carried out by Diamantino Fernandes Trindade. So much extraordinary phenomena occurred that the authors concluded they needed to unite both materials into a cohesive whole. It was evident to them that the ancestral guardians of these traditions were interested in shedding light on Vodou in their national territory since, at that point, the Brazilian publishing market only had works that fell into one of two categories: poor but popular works that did not even remotely reflect what Vodou is, and excellent academic works for a scholarly audience, dedicated to university research of the traditions of the African diaspora.

This work, therefore, does something different. While we intend to shed light on the many deceptions that shroud the beauty and mystery of Vodou, this book is not an exhaustive, sophisticated compendium of such a complex subject. Instead, it is a short manual that will provide sufficient information for first contact and can subsidize and guide future studies. If you so choose, you may look to the book's bibliography for more resources.

Read this book, then read it again, and study it carefully. It is better to know little about a subject but with well-established and solid foundations, guided by a living and legitimate tradition, than to try—and fail—to absorb a lot of information at once.

CHAPTER 1
HAITI'S BRIEF
HISTORICAL RECORD

In 1492, Christopher Columbus arrived on the island of Hispaniola and marveled at the gold ornaments displayed by the ethnic Taino natives of the tremendous Arawak nation. However, the island's gold ran out about fifty years after its discovery, leaving the island practically forgotten, inhabited by a few Spaniards, and used as a stopping point for pirates.

In 1697, half of the island was passed to France under the Treaty of Ryswick, and very quickly the French realized that the fertile soil of that land was even more valuable than the gold it once housed. This is how a massive import of enslaved Africans came to work in the fields of coffee, sisal, and sugarcane on the newly baptized island of Santo Domingo (known to the French as Saint-Domingue).

The horrors of slavery should be well-known to the reader, so it is not necessary to detail all of the strenuous work, torture, abuse, humiliation, and oppression that people of color suffered. As in Brazil and the Americas, Black people of various ethnicities, languages, and religions arrived in Santo Domingo, and property owners separated Black families in order to avoid conspiring and rebellion.

Over time, Black people created a system to serve the deities of their original lands, which they called *Règlement*. The Congolese gods of Southwest Africa came to be honored side-by-side with the Lwas (Loas) of the Fon and Ewe ethnic groups of Dahomey (present-day Benin) and the Nigerian Orishas. At the same time, some religious customs of the indigenous people of the island were incorporated, as in the case of the famous veves (attributed to the spirits and drawn on the ground with corn flour, with origins in the indigenous practice of sand painting)[2] as well as the irreverent and markedly sexual personalities of the *Ghedes* (inherited from the spirits of the dead of the Arawak and Taino cultures). Finally,

2. Although this is a thesis recorded in many books and articles on the subject, it is controversial, like practically everything related to Vodou. Thus, it is important to keep in mind that there may be other origins for the veves. Some scholars believe veves derive from the Bantu custom of using various materials to draw lines that reflect the very nature of the offered or invoked spirit.

in this cultural menagerie, French Catholicism occupied a place of maximum prominence. Enslaved people used the Catholic saints to mask the Lwa in an effort to maintain their practice undisturbed; over time, Catholic ceremonies such as baptism and marriage were incorporated, as well as the attribution of saints to the Lwas and worshipped spirits. Thus, Vodou[3] (or Haitian Vodou) was born.

It did not take long for white people to start fearing the powers of Vodou. Enslaved Africans were prohibited from dancing, though dance is a crucial component of ritual. Thus, the most famous Mambos and Houngans were killed to serve as an example to others.[4] During this time of maximum oppression, between 1751 and 1758, a runaway enslaved Houngan named François Mackandal led a rebellion that killed about six thousand white people. Mackandal was an expert in herbology and distributed

---

3. The correct spelling is *Vaudou*, but here we opted for the spelling in current use in the English language to help with correct pronunciation. Although the spelling *Voodoo* is also common, some Vodouists consider it a corruption of American Hoodoo. In Portuguese, the correct spelling of the word is *Vodu*.

4. Mambo and Houngan are female and male Voodoo priests, respectively. It is common to find the *Houngan* spelling in texts written in English, which is why it is better known. Although both spellings are correct, the word *Oungan* is usually considered more accurate to the Haitian Creole (Kreyòl) language, with the spelling *Ougan* also being accepted.

a potent poison to his coreligionists that, after being put in food and drink, caused several French families to die after experiencing excruciating pain and vomiting blood. Mackandal was eventually captured and tortured. It is said that before being burned alive, Mackandal turned into a mosquito and flew away from his executioners.

Forty years later, another Houngan tried to free the enslaved: Dutty Boukman, who, on the night of August 14, 1791, celebrated a ceremony in Bois Caïman (*Bwa Kayiman*) in which a sow was sacrificed, and according to tradition, the mighty Erzulie Dantor was first manifested. Thus, a revolt began in which it is estimated that, by the end of the first day, about two thousand white people had been killed. However, the movement lasted a short time and was harshly reprimanded, with Boukman being one of the first to be captured and executed.

Shortly afterward, in August 1793, a French commissioner named Léger-Félicité Sonthonax abolished slavery on the island, most likely to allow freed Black people to assist France in regaining local control, for the English had taken advantage of the revolution of 1791 to invade Santo Domingo. It was in this context that the first Black general emerged, the national hero Toussaint L'Ouverture. He was freed in 1777, could read and write, and spoke three languages. More importantly,

L'Ouverture had the ability to be heard in a crowd and to influence others.

L'Ouverture commanded a large battalion of formerly enslaved people under the French flag, expelled the English from the island, and was proclaimed governor of Santo Domingo. In 1801, he conquered the other part of the island, Hispaniola, abolishing slavery there and becoming the territorial governor. L'Ouverture wrote to Napoleon and asked to be inaugurated as governor with the pompous ceremony that the title called for, but the emperor saw this will as a threat to French power on the island. Napoleon sent his brother-in-law, Le Clerc, and twenty thousand men to Santo Domingo on a mission to capture L'Ouverture and reestablish slavery. L'Ouverture was arrested in 1802, deported to France, and imprisoned in a cell, where he died shortly afterward.

But the Black people of Santo Domingo had tasted freedom, and they would not so easily yield to Napoleon's attempts to reestablish slavery. There was a great revolt of the Black population, who felt betrayed by the colonizer in whose name they had fought against English invasion. In this intense period of revolt, one of L'Ouverture's generals, Jean-Jacques Dessalines, led a new rebellion, expelling French troops and proclaiming the island's independence in 1804. The land came to be known as Haiti (*Ayiti* in Kreyòl), the name the Tainos have called it since time immemorial. Two years later, Dessalines was deposed and killed, and Henri Christophe and Alexandre Pétion assumed power, the first founding a kingdom to the north and the second a republic to the south. From there, Haiti's history goes through a succession of dictatorial governments, among them Jean-Pierre Boyer, Paul Magloire, François Duvalier (Papa Doc), and Jean-Claude Duvalier (Baby Doc).

CHAPTER 2
THE VODOU THEOLOGY

The word *Vodou* evokes exotic, bewitching images: zombies wandering through a graveyard at night, pins stuck in dolls to hurt an enemy many miles away, priests cutting a chicken's throat and drinking the blood, worshippers around a campfire, etc. For many of us, perceptions about Vodou are shaped by movies we have seen and books we have read. But in reality, Vodou is not a mysterious, sinister, secret practice. On the contrary, it is an important religion, with roots as old as Africa and with millions of followers today.

Vodou originated in the Haitian West Indies during the French colonial period and is still widely practiced in Haiti. The foundations of Vodou are the tribal religions of West Africa, brought to Haiti by enslaved peoples during the seventeenth century. The word *Vodou* derives from *Vodun* in the Fon language of Dahomey, which means "spirit," "ancestor," and "deity." Haiti has been isolated for much of its history, thus allowing Vodou to develop its unique traditions, beliefs, and gods.

Enslaved Haitians were captured from many different ethnic groups throughout West Africa. These tribes shared several fundamental beliefs: serving the spirits of the family's ancestors; the use of singing, drumming, and dancing in religious rituals; and the belief that followers were possessed by immortal souls.

Once living in Haiti, the enslaved people created a religion based on their shared beliefs while absorbing the solid traditions and gods of each tribe and ethnicity. The influence of the native indigenous population in Haiti was also integrated during this formative period. For many enslaved Africans, such spiritual traditions and practices provided a vital means of mental and emotional resistance to bitter hardship.

Africans did not all speak the same language or share the same culture and religion. Since the Fon people did not speak Bantu languages, the Sudanese did not speak Fon, and the Yoruba only communicated in their own language, the language of Vodou became Kreyòl (or Haitian Creole), which was initially French with an African accent. A shared language allowed oppressed Black people to unite and identify the common elements that joined them, instead of remaining separated by their differences. Thus, a system of worship emerged that honored the customs and deities of all the African tribes and civilizations that had landed on the continent.

This new religion, called Vodou or *Sèvis Ginen* ("Service of Guinea"), is a family faith whose primary function is to recall the customs of the Black people who left Africa by force. Gathered in subhuman conditions in a strange land and leaving behind their cultural identities, they came to call Africa *Guinea* or *Ginen*, a mythical continent where their ancestors resided and where they would one day return. Vodou is a remembrance religion.

Indeed, although their beliefs and rituals may not have set them free, the Africans successfully frightened their captors. White plantation owners forbade enslaved people from practicing their native religions by threatening them with torture and death and baptized them all as Catholics. Catholicism became superimposed on African rites and beliefs, but the enslaved still practiced Vodou in secret or masked it as harmless dance.

Practitioners of this new religion added Catholic saints to their rites to hide their real faith from enslavers, and they included Catholic hymns, prayers, images, candles, and sacred relics in their rituals. Uniting French Catholicism with the original rites of all these African peoples, the *Sèvis Ginen* follows the sequence of the invocatory prayer called *Priye Ginen*, which begins with traditional Catholic prayers such as the Creed, Our Father, Holy Mary, and the Angelus, followed by the greeting to Lwa Rada and Petro.

Today, middle-class and upper-class Haitians have almost wholly abandoned Vodou beliefs and practices—at least publicly. Vodou is widely practiced by the peasant class, which encompasses most Haitians. It also migrated with Haitians to other parts of the world, with particularly strong communities in New Orleans, Miami, Charleston, and New York, with each of these communities creating new rituals and practices. Worldwide, Vodou has more than fifty million followers. Several theological systems, with their spirits, dances, rituals, and musical styles, merged into Vodou. One cannot even assume that there is uniformity in the Vodou practice on the island of Haiti, because depending on the most striking cultural influence in a particular region, there are variations in the *Règlement*.

One of the African nations that greatly influenced Vodou was the Congolese, with its sophisticated view of the world. For the Congolese, there are four basic movements in the universe, symbolized in the apparent movement of the sun around the earth and reflected in human life:

1 | The sunrise corresponds to incarnation in the physical plane;

2 | Noon relates to the maturity of adult life;

3 | Evening and sunset to old age;

4 | And midnight, death.

At that moment, the sun goes to the underground world, *Anba Dlo*, or "under the waters." It is a time of rest, recovery, and reflection. The other world, called *Kalunga*, is the world of the dead. The enormous body of water that Africans encountered when they came to America was identified with Kalunga, a relationship strengthened by the numerous deaths that occurred during the crossing, with the bodies thrown into the sea. This made the relationship between death and water stronger. It is in the realm of water that the dead await their rebirth or their journey to *Ginen*.

The Ibo nation contributed to the idea of a creator God far from humanity, which was left under the care of a myriad of spirits. The famous *govis* and *canaris*, receptacles for the Lwa and the dead, respectively, originated in the traditions of these people. The Nagos of West Africa, in turn, contributed to the military aspects that distinguish Vodou and whose main expression is the Rara parade, the carnival of peasants, which are also called "armed" and are led by generals and majors. When their bands meet along the way, they simulate a beautiful battle with singing, dancing, and rhythmic drumbeats. One striking influence of the Nagos is the satin flag used in Vodou temples, called *drapô* (*dwapo*), indicating the main

Lwa worshipped in the house. Another African nation that greatly influenced Vodou was Dahomey. The main names of the Lwa, like Agassou, Ayizan, Damballah Wedo, Ogou, Guédé, Sobo, Agwé, Atibon Legba, Bossou, etc., come from Dahomey, present-day Benin.

All Vodou ceremonies begin by pouring a little water on the temple floor to assist the arrival of spirits, alluding to the fact that just as Black people came from Africa to America by water, it will be by water that the Lwas will arrive. The watery nature of the human body, too, makes the phenomenon of possession possible. The Lwas thus manifest themselves in the waters of the ocean crossing, in the water poured on the temple floor, and in the water of the body of the faithful. It cannot be emphasized enough that water is the central element of *Sèvis Ginen*. It is poured onto the ground so that the Lwas can walk; it is offered as a gift to the Divine, who blesses it; and it is sprinkled on the assembly for cleansing and comfort purposes. The purpose of the ritual is to lead the faithful through the mythical waters of return to the abyssal waters where the ancestors, the Lwas, and the Mysteries reside. It is the return to *Ginen*.

Another central element of the practice is the *Priye Ginen*. Some elements of this long prayer are always the same; however, presentation, function, and interpretation can vary widely from temple to temple. The *Priye Ginen* is a lengthy recitation, learned by heart, that greets all the African nations that participated in the formation of Vodou. It also establishes the order of service with the sequence of the invoked Lwas and Mysteries, beginning with a litany composed of Catholic prayers and hymns in French, called *Priye Litanie*. The *Priye Djo* follows, sung in Kreyòl, in which the saints, Lwas, and ancestors worshipped in the temple are invoked. At some points, *langaj* is used, words that apparently have no meaning, coming from African dialects that ended up being lost over time or corrupted.

It is essential to keep in mind that Vodou is a monotheistic religion. In it, there is a supreme God—*Bon Dieu* or *Bondyê*—below which are the ancestors (*Zanset-yo*). Next are the Lwas or Mysteries (the word *Loa* or *Lwa* means "law" but is associated with the idea of spirits). Only the *Bondyê* is the object of worship as the Unknowable Source and the all-encompassing whole. The Lwas are served since they occupy an extremely high and relevant position in the spiritual hierarchy and can even take the petitions of the faithful directly to God. Below the Lwas are the *Guédés* or *Ghedes*, the dead in general. Finally, there are the living or incarnated.

God (*Bondyê*)

Ancestors

Mysteries: Lwa, saints, angels

Ghedes

The living

Contrary to prejudicial beliefs, Vodou theology is quite sophisticated. The soul, for example, is divided into five parts: *Gro Bon Anj*, *Ti Bon Anj*, *Met Tet*, *Nanm*, and *Zetwal*.

The *Gro Bon Anj*, literal translation a "great good angel," is the vital spark, the divine particle that keeps us alive. In esotericism, this is called the *etheric double*. Better explained, the physical body—the vehicle of consciousness with which each person has the most contact while incarnated in the material universe—presents a very subtle counterpart, invisible to the naked eye and, perhaps for this very reason, not yet identified by modern science. It appears to be made up of a very subtle energy, but not of such a quality that it can be considered spiritual; it is energy belonging to the physical dimension, and consequently, its material nature makes this subtle energy body a temporary vehicle of consciousness that disintegrates, more or less completely, at the time of the death of the physical body. *Gro Bon Anj* also includes the coarser layers of the astral body, also known as the soul, spiritual body, psychosoma, perispirit, and plastic mediator.

The *Ti Bon Anj*, literally "good little angel," is the eternal principle of the human being, in which memory and will reside. This part presents itself to God and the Lwas after death and reincarnates.

Met Tet, "my head," is the guardian angel figure, or what esoteric tradition calls the Overself. The *Met Tet* helps the *Ti Bon Anj* plan their new incarnation and helps them fulfill the assigned tasks once incarnated. All of us have a *Met Tet* (ruling spirit) that is with us from birth. However, followers are free to serve whichever Lwa they choose. There are many forms of service to the Lwa, and there are no limits upon whom a practitioner can call.

Nanm is "the vital principle" and the vitality or genetic memory inherited from ancestors. In current terms, it can also be understood as DNA. Ancient Western philosophers regarded this energy as the quintessence of the four primordial elements—earth, water, air, and fire—and named it *ether*. This same energy is called *prana* by the Hindus, *chi* by the Chinese, *ki* by the Japanese, *magnetic fluid* by Franz Anton Mesmer, *vital fluid* by Allan Kardec, and *orgone* by Wilhelm Reich, among other titles.

Zetwal, "the star" or "the destiny," resides outside the body, just like a star in the sky. *Zetwal* lives in a cosmic ocean with other stars and watches over a person's destiny. It is what theosophy calls *monad*. It is the source from which the Higher Self emanates, and little can be said about it, only that it is the closest metaphysical concept of divinity that a human being can attain. It is the "divine spark" some traditions speak of.

Two other important concepts are *Lwa Met Tet* and *Lwa Rasin*. The first, meaning "Lwa of my head," is the entity that vibrates in the frequency of the person and has more in common with them. Each person is, in a way, the earthly face of its *Lwa Met Tet*. *Lwa Rasin*, on the other hand, is linked to a person's bloodline and to their ancestors. This can be a spirit connected to the land the family inhabits or has inhabited, or even one of the founding ancestors of the family. For example, in a Black or indigenous family, a person may have the spirit of a native or an African as their *Lwa Rasin*.

Finally, we must briefly discuss the *Wonsinyon*, the spirits that accompany the *Lwa Met Tet* and somehow modify their frequency. These spirits are not exactly a person's ancestors, but spirits attached to them. Drawing a parallel with Umbanda or Kimbanda (to simplify the understanding of the concepts presented here, although it is not possible to make an exact transposition between them), one can consider the *Lwa Rasin* a spiritual guide, the one responsible for the spirituality of the medium, whereas the *Wonsinyon* would be all the other spirits that manifest through it.

A Vodouist, therefore, may have Agwe as their *Lwa Met Tet* but, at the same time, be frequently possessed by

La Sirene, Erzulie, or Ogou—or by all of them. Still, the *Lwa Met Tet* will always be the leader of the spirits who live with that particular believer.

The Traditional Worship Structure

The Vodouist temple, called *ounfò* or *honfour*, consists of a simple structure, although richly decorated with everything that the artistic streak inherent in the Haitian people can conceive; basically, an *ounfò* will consist of a place covered by a ceiling or roof, with or without walls, and another outdoor space.[5]

The covered part is called the peristyle (*péristyle*). There will always be a central mast relevant to the practice, called *poteau-mitan*, which symbolically represents a tree whose crown touches the sky and whose roots extend to the underworld. Frater Vameri, in a specific text on the subject, describes the *poteau-mitan*:

> The *poteau-mitan* is a central pole set on a base called Pe. This pole is the link between the visible and invisible world. It represents a tree with its crowns in the heavens and its roots in hell. It is usually adorned with images of Damballah and Ayida and other

5. In rural areas, temples without walls are common, which is not the case, for obvious reasons, in urban centers, where it is common to place the temple below ground in order to ensure greater freshness.

symbols. By this pole, the Lwas "descend" and "ascend" from the temple. It may have inspiration from oil palm since, for the Yoruba, this tree would be the Axis-Mundi. The cane that Papa Legba carries would be the *poteau-mitan* itself, indicating the intrinsic connection between the messenger and the "bridge" between the worlds.[6]

Inside the peristyle, Lwas altars created for both categories (Rada and Petro) are still found, but their quantity, layout, and decoration vary enormously from temple to temple. In fact, except for the peristyle, an essential element of worship found in all temples, everything else is subject to regional and even personal changes of each family of Vodou adherents. By way of illustration, Vodou is like Brazil's Afro-diasporic practices, including Umbanda, Kimbanda, Candomblé, and Batuque: although there is a bit of unity in the practice, for they will always have essential fundamentals, there will be considerable differences in less-relevant or even secondary aspects.

Concerning this liturgical diversity, well-represented in the many different versions of the altars for the Rada and Petro Lwas, the exhibition of Mambo Vye Zo Komande LaMenfo favors a more comprehensive under-

---

6. Vameri, "Templo e ferramentas do Vodou."

standing, as she points out that each temple displays its African legacy. The Rada altar presents a layered structure embellished with shining textiles and glass, cloaked in white materials that signify their esteemed ancestors. Ancestral figures originating from Africa, held in reverence as forebears, are linked to the color white, symbolizing their unblemished purity and significance. On the contrary, the Petro altars emanate a vivid crimson hue, illustrating the island's turbulent history of slavery, utilizing chains, lashes, and signals as essential components of its representation.[7]

As for the external space, usually surrounded by trees, it is used for ceremonies when the number of attendees do not all fit inside the peristyle; for services for the *Ghedes*, since some temples structure their foundations in this place and not inside the peristyle; as well as for get-togethers among family members after the rituals.

Finally, the temple also has rooms that may or may not adjoin to the peristyle called *Djevo*, intended for the seclusion of those who are undergoing the initiation processes of worship. Such rooms are equated to sacred chambers where the birth of the new initiates and priests of Vodou will take place at the end of the religious confinement, which we will discuss soon.

---

7. LaMenfo, *Serving the Spirits*.

Hierarchy and Rites of Passage

Vodou has a definite hierarchy and established rites of passage, but it cannot be said that all temples follow the same pattern. It is essential to keep in mind, therefore, that the differences and variations found from temple to temple can in no way be taken into account as disregard for tradition, but rather should be understood as part of the wealth of religion and a reflection of the principle that every family is sovereign in its Vodou temple.

As Mambo Vye Zo Komande LaMenfo rightly points out, the absence of a pope in Vodou is clear, as the foundational belief of all Vodou priests revolves around the essential principle of having the freedom to express their service.[8] Nothing exposed in this chapter should be taken as absolute truth but only as an exposition, in general terms, of what can be mentioned publicly about the customs of some temples.

It is also important to note that because Catholicism is very intertwined with the African foundations of Vodou, the temple's calendar usually brings common elements to the liturgical year of the Catholic Church. Moreover, syncretism between the Lwas and the saints of Catholic hagiography led to the commemoration of the feasts of these saints as a day to serve the Lwa attached to them. An example is the celebration of the Day of Kings

---

8. LaMenfo, *Serving the Spirits*.

(the three Magi) in praise of Simbi. On the other hand, the Congolese concept of the human being as having a beginning, a middle, and an end is expressed in the rites of *Baptem*, *Kanzo*, and in mortuary rituals such as *Anba Dlo* and *Casa Canari*.

It is common to find the description of the first rite able to make someone a Vodouist in fact and in law as *Lave Tet* and even as *Sevis Tet*, but this does not seem to us completely accurate. The *Lave Tet* ("head wash") is a rite that involves washing the person's head with specific herbs and water. In contrast, the *Sevis Tet* ("head service") or *Mange Tet* ("feed head") consist of placing elements of the mineral, vegetable, and animal kingdoms on the person's head, symbolically feeding it. It turns out that a person may need to submit to *Lave Tet* and even *Sevis Tet* without necessarily wanting to properly initiate in Vodou. Both rites are used to treat or alleviate physical and emotional problems, sort of like the *Bori* ceremony performed in Candomblé, which can be administered even to noninitiates.

The first rite of passage of the Vodou, thus, would be the *Baptem*, which comprises the *Lave Tet*, the *Mange Tet*, and the *Kouche Lwa* as well as a period of recollection, usually a day. Usually, in *Baptem* (or Baptism), the Lwa that rules the adept is defined (*Lwa Met Tet*) or the adept has a first impression of which Lwas are closest to them. The baptized adept, whose denomination is *Hounsi*, can remain in this category for the rest of their life, either because they are satisfied to be the servant of their head Lwa or because they are not destined to embrace the priesthood. Sometimes, this is a matter of money—initiations are expensive. It is important to note that Vodou can be practiced and the Lwa can be served even if a practitioner has not completed any rites of passage.

The next rite of passage is the *kanzo*,[9] which involves a longer period of recollection focused on formation and becoming a priest; this lasts twenty-one days on average. During the gathering of the *kanzo*, the person is submitted to rites that cannot be described here because they translate into internal foundations of worship. In the temples linked to the tradition of the *asson*, the ritual rattle used for the call of the Lwas, there are two priestly stages: *Sur Pwen* or *Sipwen* (Priest or Assistant Priestess) and *Asogwe* (bearer of the *asson*) Priest or Priestess, who hold the authority to have their own house in Vodou. Note that not all aspects of Vodou make use of *asson*, and there are very traditional families in Haiti that do not use it.

Another typical ceremony is *Maraj Lwa*, the Lwa wedding. It occurs when the Lwa of a Vodouist requests to establish a stronger bond or when two Lwas express the desire to marry, further intensifying the family bond and initiation between the participants in this marriage.

---

9. Some houses comprise *Baptem* as an integral part and the first stage of *kanzo*.

In Vodou, the Priestess is called *Mambo. Houngan* (sometimes called *Gangan*) is the male denomination for Priest. The term is derived from the Fon *hùn gan*. Mambos and Houngans conduct the rituals and evoke the Lwas. The Houngan practicing black magic is called *Bakor* or *Boko*, and a Mambo, in turn, is known as *Caplata*.

Finally, after this brief overview, it is necessary to remember that submission to the rites of passage within Vodou establishes a solemn commitment to worship and an unbreakable bond between the Lwas and the adept. Both a *hounsi* and a Priest or Priestess submit to severe oaths and become servants of the Lwas. The most significant difference between the *hounsi* and the one who holds the priestly degree is that the first is the servant of their head Lwa (*Lwa Met Tet*), while the second surrenders to the service of the other Lwas of the Vodouist pantheon.

Priye Ginen

The *Priye Ginen* is a popular Haitian prayer used in Vodou ritual openings. The prayer—an icon of the symbiosis between the Christian and African cosmology that developed in the country—mixes elements of popular Catholicism and traditions from Africa, simultaneously invoking the protection of the Christian God, several Catholic saints, and the ancestral Lwas divinized that would have the faculty to be present among the faithful through the possession of one of their devotees.

This is not a full version of the *Priye Ginen* and is meant to show the uninitiated how this invocation proceeds. This version of the *Priye Ginen* was taught to Mambo Samantha Corfield, Bon Mambo Feraye de la Kwa Daginen, in Haiti at her initiation, though there can be subtle differences from one Vodou house to another.[10]

> *We pray the Lord's Prayer, the Hail Mary, and the Apostles' Creed.*
> *The officiant shall continue:*
>
> > *L'ange de Seigneur dit a Marie*
> > *Qu'elle concevoit en Jesus Christ*
> > *(Jezukri)*
> > *La Trinite lui a choisi*
> > *Elle est Concu du Saint Esprit*[11]
>
> *The congregation claps ten times.*
>
> > *Venez mon Dieu venez*
> > *Venez mon doux Sauveur*
> > *Venez regne en mol*

---

10. Visit www.spellmaker.com to learn more about Mambo Samantha Corfield.

11. The angel of the Lord said to Mary / That it will be conceived in Jesus Christ / The Trinity chose him (for her) / It is the *Concu* (conclusion/decision) of the Holy Mind.

Au center du mon Coeur
Venez mon Dieu Venez.[12]

The congregation claps ten times.

Vous qui vivez dans la souffrance
Faites de toujours votre devoir
Ne courez pas en desespoir
La gloire de Dieu couronne
    l'esperance[13]

The congregation claps ten times.

Grace Marie Grace
Jesus Pardonez Nous[14]

The group sings the next verse. In New Orleans Voodoo, "The Atibon Legba" song is sung here.

Sen Pierre ouvert la porte
Sen Pierre ouvert la porte pou moi
Sen Pierre ouvert la porte
La porte pou paradise[15]

---

12. Come my God come / Come my soft Savior / Come rule/reign in soft / In the center of my Heart / Come my God Come.

13. You who live in suffering / Make of always your duty (do what you are supposed to do) / Do not run in fear/despair / The glory of God crowns the matter/story/experience.

14. Grace Mary Grace / Jesus forgive us.

15. Saint Peter open the door / Saint Peter open the door for me / Saint Peter open the door / The door to paradise.

After this verse for Saint Peter, one can follow many other verses, which vary from temple to temple and are usually taught to members at the time of their initiation. In a group, the officiant will call the names of the saints and the Lwas, and the group will give the same answer every time. First, the saints are called:

> **Officiant:** *Avec* _____
> **Group:** *Sen Djo-e*
>   (phonetically SAHN JO-AY)
> **Officiant:** *Avec* _____
> **Group:** *Sen Djo-e du ko agwe*
>   (phonetically SAHN JO-AY
>   DO KOH AHGWAY)
> **Officiant:** *Et Avec* _____
> **Group:** *Lavi nan men bondye-o sen.*
>   (phonetically LAVEE NAHN
>   MEHN BOND YAY-OH
>   SEHN)

The text above is the same to call the complete list of saints and Lwas. The officiant says "I am with" or "we are with," which is said as "with" (avec) followed by the name of each saint or Lwa. The answer is a bit more complicated.

Sen Djo-e *is interpreted in some temples as "Saints and Angels," but there is some con-*

troversy about the translation, for these words are langaj, *that is, words whose exact meaning has been lost.*

Sen Djo-e du ko agwe *is a little clearer, meaning "Saints and Angels under the waters" or "Saints and Angels in the waters." Here, in this part of the prayer, the reference is not to Agwé, the great Lwa of the waters, but to water itself—even though the word in Kreyòl for water is* dlo.

Lavi nan men bondye-o sen *means "life is in the hands of the Good God, the Holy One." When using a rattle or* asson, *it is held in the right hand.*

> *Father* [*Dieu la Pere*, "God, the
>   Father"]
> *Jezukri* [Jesus Christ, the son]
> *Holy Spirit*
> *Virgin Mary*
> *St. Peter*
> *St. Anthony*
> *St. Lazarus*
> *St. Cosmos*
> *St. Damien*
> *St. Paul*
> *St. Joseph*

St. Ulrich
Moses
St. Vincent de Paul
St. Isidore
St. Jacques Majeur
Rele tout sen-gason dan lesyel.
Rele tout sen songe tou sen pa songe.[16]

Now the female saints are called:

Officiant: *Avec _____*
Group: *Sen Djo-e*
Officiant: *Avec _____*
Group: *Sen Djo-e du ko agwe*
Officiant: *Et Avec _____*
Group: *Lavi nan men bondye-o sen.*
   St. Philomene
   St. Claire
   St. Elizabeth
   Our Lady of Immaculate
      Conception
   St. Martha
   Our Lady of Charity
   Holy Virgin
   Matre Dolorosa
   St. Mary Magdelene
   Rele tout famn-sint-yo nan

---

16. Hear our prayer, all the male saints in heaven. / All the male saints I named and those and those I have forgotten.

> *lasyel.*
> *Tout sent songe et tout sent pa songe.*[17]

The following verse is sung between each litany when reference to the Lwas begins:

> **Group:** *Lisa badjye*
> *Oungan siye*
> *Lisa Dole Zo*
> **Officiant:** *Eh-zo*
> *Zo li mache li mache li mache*
> *Zo li mache dol mache nan*
> *Lavi nan men bondye o Sen-yo*

This verse means that one is entering the Kingdom of Guinea as the group prepares to call the Lwas. Zo *is the Dahomey word for "fire."* Lisa *is the male half of the ancient deity of Dahomey named* Mawu-Lisa *(the Divine Twins), the origin of the Marassa, the Vodou twin Lwas.* Li mache *means to march or walk on fire.*

The Lwa Rada are called.

> **Officiant:** *Avec* _____
> **Group:** *Sen Djo-e*
> **Officiant:** *Avec* _____

---

17. Hear our prayer, all the female saints of heaven. / All those named and those not named.

Group: *Sen Djo-e du ko agwe*
Officiant: *Et Avec* _____
Group: *Lavi nan men bondye-o sen*

Legba

Marassa

Loko

Ayizan

Damballah

Ayida Ouedo

Sobo

Badesy

Agasou

Silibo

Agwe

LaSiren

Ezili

Bosou

Agaou

Azaka

Ogoun St. Jacques

Ogoun Badagris

Ogoun Ferraille

Ogoun Shango

Ogoun Balindjo

Rele tout Lwa-yo dan lasyel.

Tout Lwa-yo songe et tout Lwa-yo
pa songe.[18]
Group: *Lisa badjye*
Oungan siye
Lisa Dole Zo
Officiant: *Eh-zo*
Zo li mache li mache li mache
Zo li mache dol mache nan
Lavi nan men bondye o Sen-yo.

At this time, the Realm of the Dead is evoked, the Ghede, *and the Baron. This is done between the call of the Rada and Petro Lwas to show that the* Ghede *are the bridge between Rada and Petro.*

At this point in the Priye, *the asson is put down and a rattle* (tcha-tcha) *is used. This is held in the leader's left hand.*

Officiant: *Avec* _____
Group: *Sen Djo-e*
Officiant: *Avec* _____
Group: *Sen Djo-e du ko agwe*
Officiant: *Et Avec* _____
Group: *Lavi nan men bondye-o sen.*
Ghede

---

18. Hear our prayer, all the Lwa in Heaven. / All the Lwa I have named and all Lwa I have not named.

Baron Samedi
Baron LaCroix
Maman Gran Brigitte
Ghede Brav
Ghede La Vie
Ghede Fatra
Ghede Mazaka
Ghede Nibo
Pou tout mort-yo ki mwen rele.
Et tout mort-yo ki mwen pa rele.[19]

At this point, the drumming changes, becoming faster, to indicate that one will enter the domains of the Petro Lwas. Everyone sings and claps:

Toni rele Congo
Toni rele Congo
Toni rele Congo
Santa Maria gras ya
Aye Santa Maria ya
Aye Santa Maria ya
Aye Santa Maria ya
Santa Maria Gras ya
Toni rele Congo
Toni rele Congo
Toni rele Congo
Santa Maria gras ya

---

19. For all the dead I have named. / For all the dead I have not named.

These verses are often repeated during the possessions, which often occur at this time. The verses translate to, basically, "Everyone listen (or hear us) in the Congo" and "Hurray for Santa Maria (Mary)," asking her to give us thanks and bless us.

Now the Petro Lwas are called:

> **Officiant:** *Avec_____*
> **Group:** *Sen Djo-e*
> **Officiant:** *Avec _____*
> **Group:** *Sen Djo-e du ko agwe*
> **Officiant:** *Et Avec _____*
> **Group:** *Lavi nan men bondye-o sen.*
> > *Legba Petro*
> > *Marassa Petro*
> > *Wangol*
> > *Ibo*
> > *Senegal*
> > *Kongo*
> > *Kaplaou*
> > *Kanga*
> > *Takya*
> > *Zoklimo*
> > *Simbi Dlo*
> > *Gran Simba*
> > *Kalfu*
> > *Simitye*
> > *Granbwa*

Kongo Savann
Ezili Danto
Marinette
Don Petro
Ti-Jean Petro
Simbi Andezo
Simbi Makaya
Rele tout Lwa-yo dan lasyel.
Tout Lwa-yo songe et tout Lwa-yo
*   pa songe.*[20]

Group: *Lisa badjye*
Oungan siye
Lisa Dole Zo

Officiant: *Eh-zo*
Zo li mache li mache li mache
Zo li mache dol mache nan
Lavi nan men bondye o Sen-yo
Mwen soti la priere pou Mystere
*   la yo.*[21]

⁓ ᴑ · ᴑ ⁓

---

20. Hear our prayer, all the Lwa in Heaven. / All Lwa I have named and all Lwa I have not named.

21. I leave a prayer for the Mysteries (the Lwa).

Do you want to hear a full version of the *Priye Ginen* performed by the group Roots of Haiti? Visit the link in the footnote to listen now![22]

The Ghedes

Haitian Vodou has a class of spirits called *Ghede*,[23] patrons of cemeteries and death. *Ghede* is a family of spirits expressing death and fertility powers. These spirits are as much about life as death, for without life, there is no death. The *Ghede* is a spiritual family (nation or *nachon*) that can be worshipped by anyone, regardless of whether they have been initiated or not.

The origin of the *Ghedes* is controversial. Some hold that Papa Loko, as the first Houngan, removed the first *Ghede* from the waters of death. Others say that the first *Ghede* and originator of this large family was Baron Samedi himself, which will be discussed shortly. Just like Vodou practitioners, anthropologists have varying opinions. Some scholars contend that the origins of *Ghede* can be linked to the indigenous Arawak and Taino peoples. On the other hand, some suggest that their beginnings lie

---

22. https://www.youtube.com/watch?v=z38lSOM8SSQ

23. One can also write Gédé or Guédé (the phonetics of the word respect French grammar).

in Gede-Vi, an African tribe that no longer exists due to a pre-enslavement conflict.[24]

Neves cites that *Ghede* appear dressed as funeral directors, with old overcoats and top hats, with their faces covered in rice powder and often wearing sunglasses;[25] for example, Baron Cemitierè or Baron Samedi (*Samedi*, Saturday, the last day of Creation) is placed under the sign of Saturn and symbolized by the color black. He keeps a certain correspondence with Exu Caveira, a Kimbanda spirit assumed to be lord of cemeteries. When the *Ghede* arrive, they perform a stylized dance (*banda Gede*), choreography in which they throw their torso backward, keeping the hips projected inward, and make ellipses with the lower abdomen in a simulation of sexual acts. Not infrequently, the *Ghede* carries a staff that holds explicitly phallic characteristics. They like to make jokes, always of sexual connotation. Sex and death, Eros and Thanatos, are the forces symbolized and manifested in the *Ghedes*. They enjoy spicy drinks such as *Piman*, a mix of rum and twenty-one varieties of potent peppers. To prove the complete possession of the *cavalo* ("horse," as the Vodouist in trance is called), Vodouists can rub this mixture into their eyes and genitals, which would cause excruciating pain in anyone who was not in an altered state of consciousness.

---

24. Filan, *The Haitian Vodou Handbook*.
25. Neves, *Do Vodu à Macumba*.

Ghedes Day, November 2, All Saints' Day, is a national holiday in Haiti, celebrated with a great party, *Fèt Gede*, in which countless *Ghedes* circulate the streets playing and drinking in perfect possession of their *cavalos* ("horses"). Papa Ghede is considered the corpse of the first man who died. He is recognized as a tall Black man with a hat on his head, a cigarette in his mouth, and an apple in his left hand. He is a psychopomp that waits at the crossroads to take souls in the afterlife and also has the power to heal and ward off death.[26]

It is essential to differentiate the Lwas from the *Ghedes*. The former are manifestations of the divine laws, aspects of God (*Le Bon Dieu* or *Bondyê* in Haiti), sometimes considered intermediate angels between the divine and the human (*Les Anges* or *Zanj*), whereas the latter are spirits of people who once lived on earth. When faced with a dead person manifested in their rituals through the possession of an adept, the Vodouists used to say: "We are not before a Lwa, but a mystery!" Hence came the custom of calling the *Ghedes* "Mysteries," or *Mistès* in Kreyòl.

---

26. The word *psychopomp* originates from the Greek *psychopompos*, a combination of *psyche* (soul) and *pompos* (guide), designating an entity whose function is to guide or conduct the perception of a human being between two or more significant events.

Baron Samedi

The *Ghede* are closely associated with Ghede Baron, whose aspects are Baron Samedi (Bawon Samedi), Baron of the Cross (Bawon La Kuá or Baron La Croix), and Cemetery Baron (Bawon Cimitiè or Baron Cemitière). Depending on the tradition followed, Baron may be one of the *Ghede*; their spiritual protector, as he raises them from the dead with the help of Baron Samedi and his wife Maman Brigitte; or still, an aspect of *Ghede*. Still, the Baron usually manifests more seriously than the *Ghedes*, who some consider "children." In any of these configurations (Baron, Maman Brigitte, and the *Ghede*), their domain is death, the cemetery, and the grave. Usually, the tombs of the first man and the first woman buried in a cemetery symbolize the tombs of Baron Samedi and Maman Brigitte, respectively. Among the better-known *Ghedes* are Ghede Nibo, Brav Ghede, Ti Mazka (which manifests itself as a child), Ghede Plumaj, Ghede Zaranyen (whose shape is a spider), Ghede Souffrant, and Ghede-Nouvavou.

Mambo Vye Zo Komande LaMenfo explains the difference between the *Ghedes* and the Baron. Baron Samedi directly personifies Death. He occupies a central position within the cryptic realms of the Vodou cosmos and wields authoritative command over the thresholds of death. No *Ghede* is granted entry into this domain without obtaining clear authorization from the Baron. Frequently, the Baron is summoned to accompany the undisciplined *Ghede*, who emerge as night draws to a close to partake in the rituals of smoking and drinking.[27]

Baron Samedi's Veve

Frater Vameri explains the famous Baron Samedi, syncretized with Saint Gerald Magela, Saint Gabriel the Archangel, and Saint Expedite, as follows:

> In Vodou, Baron Samedi is one of the expressions of death. Traditionally, he is believed to manifest himself through the first dead man buried in a cemetery. He is a more severe Lwa than the other *Ghedes* (in

---

27. LaMenfo, *Serving the Spirits.*

fact, all Barons are more serious), who are usually joking and irreverent. His clothes, with his suit or tuxedo and top hat, already denote his authority. In addition, details of his clothing denote his close connection to Freemasonry, which also contributes to his aura of authority and sobriety. It could not be any different, since this spirit is death itself and not so much a dead one. Death is inevitable and always a matter of being treated with respect. However, his possessions are not always ceremonious. The Baron can present himself irreverently, only not as irreverent as the other *Ghedes*.[28]

Another interesting aspect noted in the Barons' clothing, especially Baron Samedi, is the presence of Masonic symbols. In fact, Haitian Vodou was greatly influenced by Freemasonry brought by French colonizers and esoteric movements from eighteenth- and nineteenth-century France, such as Rosicrucianism and Martinism. Thus, parallel to the popular Vodou, numerous secret Vodouist societies emerged that mixed Vodou with esoteric and gnostic currents. One of the most famous of these secret societies, still active today, is *La Couleuvre Noire* ("The Black Snake"), founded by Lucien-François Jean-Maine

---

28. Vameri, "Barão Samedi."

from his initiations in several French organizations at the hands of the famous occultist Papus (Gérard Encausse) and his high knowledge of exoteric and esoteric Vodou. Subsequently, his son, Hector-François Jean-Maine, continued his father's work, and today, *La Couleuvre Noire* is led by the American Michael Bertiaux.

Maman Brigitte

Maman Brigitte is a Lwa of death and, thus, life. She protects gravestones in cemeteries if they are correctly marked with a cross. The Vodouist calls for her when they want to somehow get justice. In religious syncretism with Catholicism, she is associated with Mary Magdalene and Saint Brigid.

Maman Brigitte's Veve

About Maman Brigitte, Frater Vameri says:

> Like this great mother of death, Brijit is also one of Vodou's judges. She acts in causes of justice and resolution, which seems very timely since legends of judgment at the time of death are abundant. Moreover, there is no equalizer more excellent than death—and this is one of the great lessons we can learn from the *Ghede*.[29]

Milo Rigaud observes that the clientele of Maman Brigitte is partially composed of individuals who are consistently engaged in disputes with their friends and neighbors, perpetually have adversaries, and are continually immersed in debates. On the journey to the cemetery, to seek guidance from the "Mystery" (regarded as the eldest among the deceased and, therefore, the wisest), the stem of a *bahayonde* (*Prosopis juliflora*, or mesquite) is cut by the client before being positioned in front of an elm. As the stem is being cut, the phrase "In the name of Mademoiselle Brigitte" is spoken. Upon reaching the tree, the following words are pronounced with significant authority: "Mademoiselle Brigitte, here lies the whip that [so-and-so] cut to attack. They are presented before

---

29. Vameri, "Manman Brijit - a dona do cemitério."

you so that you can impart the lesson they merit." If the intention is to foment discord between two individuals, the prayer must incorporate the subsequent words: "Prevent A from reconciling with B or C."[30]

Papa Legba

In Haitian Vodou, we find Papa Legba (guardian of the crossroads), an intermediary between the Lwa and humanity. Although Papa Legba is not a *Ghede*, he is the symbolic opposite because, on one hand, the *Loa Guede* personifies death, while on the other hand, he personifies life.[31]

In West Africa, Legba is a Vodun forerunner.[32] He is the Vodun of good and evil, the lord of crossroads and paths. Usually seated at the village entrance, he drives away all evil spirits. He is invoked before any ceremony to ensure the quiet and smooth running of the ritual. He is always depicted on a mound of earth and with sexual attributes above standard measurements. Between the Fon and the Éwé, Legba has a predominantly phallic aspect, and his initiates, the *Legbasi*, carry Legba's sacred tools, composed of a complex apparatus, with gourds and phallic sculptures.

---

30. Rigaud, *Secrets of Voodoo*.

31. Rigaud, *Secrets of Voodoo*.

32. Vodun is another name given to the Lwas.

Legba, guardian of temples, villages, and private houses, mounted in the form of a mound of clay from which a sizeable erect phallus emerges, is eminently an Agbo-Legba (collective entity) but is also known as the Assi-Legba (female Legba), which is worshipped to protect women and children in the community. For the Fon, Legba's wife is Awovi. In Haiti, Legba is syncretized with Saint Lazarus, and in New Orleans with Saint Peter. In short, the *Ghede*, who come from the waters of death, symbolizes physical fertility, while Legba, who comes from dry land, symbolizes virginal fertility.

In Haiti, Papa Legba owns the spiritual crossroads and gives (or denies) permission to speak to the spirits. He is the portal and is always the first and last spirit invoked at any ceremony because his authorization is necessary for communication between mortals and the Lwas. Papa Legba is responsible for bringing requests and offerings to the Vodou gods. He is a great communicator and speaks every language found on earth and amongst the deities. He alone has the power to open the door to let spirits enter the human world. All ceremonies begin with an offering to Papa Legba so he can open the door and let the spirits pass. His colors are red and black, and Papa Legba is also known as Legba Atibon and Ati-Gbon Legba ("Good Old Legba").

According to Diogo Quiareli, people are afraid of Papa Legba, but he is actually a gracious and paternal figure, and it does not take much to appease him.[33] He is not demanding, though he does love riddles since he is a trickster. Papa Legba enjoys helping people find clarity.

As stated earlier, Legba is the intermediary between the Lwas and humanity—he allows humans to speak to the Lwas. Haitian Vodou practitioners believe in a supreme creator, *Le Bon Dieu* or *Bondyê*, which means "Good God." *Bondyê* doesn't directly interfere in human affairs, so another spirit must serve as the go-between: Papa Legba. It is said that no one else will ever be able to reach Legba's level of spirituality.[34]

There are many chants that can be said to summon Papa Legba. One of them is:

> Papa Legba, open the gate for me and let me in.
> Papa Legba, open the gate for me.
> Open the gate for me, Papa,
> For me to pass. When I return, I will thank the Lwas!

Usually, Papa Legba is offered coffee, chopped tobacco, roasted corn, peanuts, sugarcane, palm oil, gin, and rum.

---

33. Quiareli, "A história de Papa Legba."
34. Quiareli, "A história de Papa Legba."

Zombies: Myth or Reality?

When the Vodou theme comes up, one of the first images that comes to people's minds is the zombie, a magically reanimated corpse used for manual labor on Haitian plantations. Most people relegate this figure to local legends and will give a polite smile, a mixture of pity and contempt, knowing that Haitians still affirm the existence of zombies, less because they believe in them than because they actually live with the phenomenon. But is the zombie myth or reality?

The answer to this question is not simple, but it can be summed up as such: it is neither one thing nor the other. In the 1980s, ethnobotanist Wade Davis spent three years studying the zombie phenomenon in Haiti. After several adventures told in his book *A Serpente E O Arco Iris* ("*The Serpent and the Rainbow*"), he discovered that the process of zombification was nothing more than a terrible poisoning technique that the *bokors* ("sorcerers") and local secret societies used as a form of revenge.

Basically, the poison was made with the toxin of a local fish, poisonous herbs, and other organic elements such as animal and human bones. The main toxin in the mixture, tetrodotoxin, is about 1,200 times more toxic than cyanide.[35] Transformed into dust, the poison was blown into the face of the victim, who, upon inhaling it,

---

35. Lago et al., "Tetrodotoxin, an Extremely Potent Marine Neurotoxin."

almost immediately suffered from a process of cerebral dullness that culminated in an unconscious state of apparent death. The victim was veiled as if dead and buried in the local cemetery, although in such a way that there was still some oxygen available. On the night of the same day, the *bokor* conducted a ceremony in which they symbolically resurrected the victim by applying a substance that revived them.[36] The brain damage caused, however, was permanent: the newly created zombie, completely stupefied, would carry out their master's orders and perform all sorts of manual labor.

Wade Davis's research posited that zombies existed in Haiti, though not quite the way they are portrayed by pop culture. Legends describe zombies as people who had their soul stolen by a spell, captured in a state of "perpetual purgatory," and were sent to work as an enslaved person on a plantation. Having a legion of zombies was never the goal; rather, the idea of losing one's soul (i.e., to a Vodouist, losing the possibility of a worthy death) was "a fate worse than death." These poisonings were handled by secret societies in rural areas and had a political role. In fact, this was the most significant punishment for those who violated "the rules of traditional culture."[37]

---

36. It is important to note that many more died than were revived.

37. Davis, *A Serpente E O Arco Iris*.

One of the cases studied by Wade Davis was that of Clairvius Narcisse, a man recognized as dead and buried in the presence of friends and family but found wandering over a decade later. After being taken to a hospital, Narcisse recounted that his zombification had been contracted with a *bokor* by his own brother, who wanted to take the family land. Wade Davis's account was so successful that, in 1987, the well-known director Wes Craven directed a film based on Davis's book, which was also called *The Serpent and the Rainbow*. The movie was released in Brazil with the not-so-happy title *A Maldição dos Mortos-Vivos* ("*The Curse of the Living Dead*").

Are you looking for more traditional Haitian Vodou songs? Visit the link in the footnote to listen to the playlist we have prepared especially for you! [38]

---

38. https://open.spotify.com/playlist/7iv5maWv3i4evzAnBOxnXf?si
=af8b7285d1bc46e6

CHAPTER 3
THE LWAS RADA AND PETRO

Vodou has a host of spiritual beings called angels, ancestors, spirits, Mysteries, and Lwas. These beings transmit the will and governance of God and bridge the communication between mankind and the Divine. Some are not human, others were once human, and others are far beyond human comprehension. The Lwas manifest themselves through possession and dreams, dividing into two large groups called Rada and Petro.

Rada are the most prominent Lwa family in Haitian Vodou and in *Règlement*; in the rule governing the Vodou rituals, they come first. Rada include benevolent spirits related to West African Voduns. The Rada Lwas come from West Africa, including the ethnic groups of Arada, Dahomey, Senegal, Ibo, and Kongo. They are seen as benevolent, cold, and sweet. Their offerings are usually white animals, molasses, *sirop d'orgeat* (almond syrup), and other sweet items. The rhythm of the Rada service, accompanied by the *asson*, is slower, and its songs are closer to sung prayers.

Next, in *Règlement*, the Petro Lwas are considered more aggressive, linked to the new world because they were born on the island of Haiti. This name is attributed to the enslaved Dom Pedro, who would have created this style of service. The Petro Lwas are known as "hot Lwas," but the sometimes-publicized distorted notion that they are evil spirits is incorrect. They are more agitated; their action is faster and more dangerous to deal with, as they are less flexible and less tolerant than the Rada Lwas. Petro Lwas are powerful, fierce sorcerers, and it is advisable to deal with them with caution. Maya Deren notes that while the Rada Lwas represent protective powers, the Petro Lwas are the patrons of aggressive action.[39] The rhythm of the Petro service, accompanied by the maraca, is faster and syncopated, and it is accompanied by the cracking of whips, whistles, and the burst of gunpowder.

Rada

Here are some of the Rada Lwas.

Papa Legba

Papa Legba, also known as Ati-bon Legba, is the guardian of the portal that separates the visible and invisible

39. Deren, *Divine Horsemen*.

worlds. Without it, no communication between the physical and spiritual planes is possible, so Legba is always the first Lwa to be revered and served in the *Règlement*. He is also the mediator between God (*Bondyê*) and all the other Lwas. As Frater Vameri observes, "He is so fundamental that even in ceremonies that a server conducts in an intimate and solitary way, at home, Papa Legba needs to be the first to be greeted," for "without the blessings of Papa Legba, not even the most direct connection with a server's personal Lwa will be possible."[40]

Papa Legba's Veve

Legba represents the Sun, the light that illuminates the world, and is considered the most important and influential among all the spirits. His role as sentinel gives

40. Vameri, "Papa Legba."

him the keys to the *poteau-mitan* (the central mast present in every *ounfò*/Vodou temple) of the invisible kingdoms, and for this reason it is therefore also known as *gran chemin* ("great route"). Regarding Papa Legba (as well as Erzulie, who will be discussed later), Milo Rigaud, an erudite writer acclaimed for his esoteric vision of Vodou, makes interesting considerations. He says that Legba, the foundational figure of Vodou, assumes the role of the Sun, presiding over rituals, while Erzulie, the primordial woman, embodies the Moon. Legba finds his parallel in Christ, and Erzulie in the Virgin Mary. The remaining Mysteries follow in a structured hierarchy. In his outward manifestation, Legba takes the form of a man who ritually sprinkles water onto the earth; this depiction is acknowledged by adept practitioners who commence each ceremony by moistening the soil. Erzulie is sometimes symbolized as an Ethiopian Black woman, her complexion a necessity due to her union with the Sun, which causes her to be "burnt." Implicit in this portrayal is a deeper significance: this remarkably dark and exquisite woman draws a connection, within the Afro-Jewish tradition, to the stunningly dark and beautiful Queen of Sheba. Consequently, the serpent, Ainda-Wédo, depicted on the walls of the *oum'phor*, takes on a new recognition, through the lens of religious syncretism, as the Ethiopian queen who journeyed to meet Solomon, renowned for constructing the Temple. By delving into these depictions, the astrological origins of the Vodou faith, along with its diverse spheres of religious influence from around the world, can be discerned with remarkable ease.[41]

Naturally, despite his solar attribution, Papa Legba carries mercurial aspects as, like Hermes and Mercury of Greco-Roman mythology, he is the intermediary between mankind and the gods. The virtues attributed to Legba are humility, wisdom, and communication, and he is traditionally represented as a very old man who limps and uses a cane or crutches. Traditionally, Legba is considered lame because he has one foot in the physical world and the other in the spirit world. His colors are white and red, and his symbols are the keys, the cane, and the crutches.

Papa Legba likes strong coffee and tobacco for his pipe. He also enjoys chicken and goat on the coals, sweet potatoes, bananas, fresh fruits in general, and sweets. The tradition associates Papa Legba with Saint Lazarus and Saint Peter, the first because he is seen as an older man using crutches, and the second because he is usually depicted carrying the keys of heaven in his hands.

Marassa

The Marassa, the sacred twins, are divine children and are older than the other Lwas, except for Papa Legba. They dwell between the worlds, filled with divine love. According

---

41. Rigaud, *Secrets of Voodoo.*

to Milo Rigaud, they are Love, Truth, Justice, and the mystery of the union between heaven and earth.[42] They also represent abundance, blessings, and all divine mysteries. Without the Marassa, nothing comes into existence.

The word *Marassa* derives from the Kikongo *Mabassa*, which means "those who come in a pair." With the Marassa comes Dosu or Dosa, the child born after the birth of twins.

They are offered sweetened coffee, sweets, sugary fried bananas, rice with red beans, rice cooked with coconut milk, and cinnamon, all in pairs.

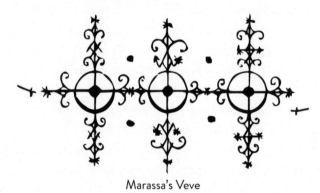

Marassa's Veve

Although there are two, the fact that they always appear united to Dosu (in a figuration similar to Cosmas, Damian, and Doum in Brazilian Umbanda) makes the number assigned to them three. Their colors are light blue

42. Rigaud, *Secrets of Voodoo*.

and light pink. In the Rada pantheon, they are syncretized with Cosmas and Damian, while in the Petro pantheon, they are associated with the Three Virtues (Faith, Hope, and Charity) and the Three Egyptian Queens.

Regarding this trine aspect of the Marassa, Frater Vameri provides essential considerations:

> Pressley-Sanon draws attention to the fact that after the twins (Marasa), a third element must come—a son after the twins. In this case, we cannot lose sight of the fact that we may be talking about triplets (Marasa twa). That is, the two twins are born, and then comes the third element. It is necessary to consider that the third element is fundamental because it is the birth of complementarity: that is, it is a representation of creation. Here, the allegories with the very creation of life, in which two add up to generate a third, are evident.
>
> This formula of one plus one generating three is what expresses the concept of the Marasa. Thus, we clearly see that they represent expansion and growth. As I have already written, they also represent a creation. So, the Marasa has a special place among the Lwas. The Marasa are considered enormously powerful and are served

soon after Papa Legba (sometimes right after Papa Loko and Ayizan). Some practitioners believe that the Marasa were created before Legba, but as he opens the gates— you need to serve him first.

Although they are represented as children, the Marassa are old and very powerful to be able to manifest themselves by possession. Their importance is such that there is considered to exist a Vodouist trinity: the Marassa, the Lwas, and the ancestors.

Papa Loko

Papa Loko, the Lwa of healing, is the father of the initiates, the just judge and healer of the temple. He plays a leading role in the initiation of the Mambos and the Houngans, for he confers the *asson*, the ritualistic rattle that distinguishes the holder of the highest initiatory rank in Vodou.

Being one of the ancient Lwas, the primordial Houngan carries knowledge about plants and herbs, remedies and cures. Loko is also recognized as an aerial spirit and is said to fly in the air like a butterfly, allowing him to enter places unnoticed and listen to people's conversations. As he knows all the dialogue between humans, Loko is an expert in issuing judgments and resolving disputes.

Papa Loko's Veve

It is interesting to note that the Taino people called themselves *Loko-no* or "Sons of Loko," the mythical founder of the Arawak nation, in which the very use of the *asson* originated according to some sources, although others associate it with royalty, wielded only by the descendants of the royal house of Dahomey (present-day Benin). Still, some experts maintain that the origin of this Lwa is African, arguing that in Dahomey, Loko would be one of the royal ancestors, served only by the priest-kings who ruled the people.

Papa Loko's colors are white, gold, yellow, and light green. He is associated with Saint Joseph since just as Joseph was the father of Jesus, the greatest initiate of the Judeo-Christian tradition, Loko is the father of all initiates. Papa Loko drinks *kleren* (a type of artisanal Haitian rum), beer, and sugary coffee. His offerings are palm oil, popcorn, rice with several types of beans, rice with mushrooms, and pumpkin soup. These offerings are placed in the *latanier*, a bag made with palm leaves and hung on its sacred tree, the *mafumeira* (*Ceiba pentandra*).

Since Papa Loko is the Lord of *Asson*, it is worth bringing some more information to this vital object of power in the Vodou temples that use it. Frater Selwanga shares relevant considerations on the subject:

> The sacred rattle of the Vodou, the *asson*, bound with beads and containing secrets, is today the holy object that identifies the *houngan* and *mambo* of Vodou. The *asson* as a symbol of *houngan* and *mambo asogwe*, however, is a testimony to the importance of creolization, since the *asson* was originally a symbol of royalty and was wielded by few people. This select group of people were those descended from the royal lineage of Dahomey (Benin). Orality tells that these priests, who are understood to be twenty-one in number, were recognized by a spiritual tool they carried with them that was called *asogwe*. The *asogwe* was a gourd rattle, the same one we now call *asson*, a word meaning a network of beads. It was these twenty-one priests who organized the

formalities of the fateful *sevi* in Bwa Kayiman in 1791, which was led by Boukman Dutty and Cecile Fatiman and which triggered the revolutionary battle for independence that lasted thirteen years….

The story of the *asson* in Vodou is a testimony to the beauty of spiritual generosity, the will to preserve memory, and the absence of spiritual selfishness by offering the royal fire of the *asson* as a means of awakening those royal powers in distant people in memory and the legacy of Guinea. This attitude gave equal status of importance to the *Lwas Rada*, the original *Lwas* of Africa, and the *Lwas Petwo*, the spiritual forces that formed in the new world, in the Haitian Vodou *Asogwe*. Vodou is fire and Vodou is water. Vodou is oil and wine fused alchemically, an impossibility made possible by the star dance of the *Lwas* casting themselves through the web of the world like beads, vertebrae, and secrets…so naturally, when the *asson* is swayed, so are the *Lwas*, and when the *Lwas* are swayed, so are we. We are swayed into the memory of Guinea that infuses us with the secret wisdom that allows us to stir the cauldron of water until it ignites! [43]

---

43. Selwanga, "O Asson no Vodou."

Ayizan

Ayizan, when paired up with Papa Loko, is the mother of the initiates; the first Mambo is seen as a much older woman wearing an apron with several pockets. She is an ancient deity of Dahomey, and her name comes from the Fon people, meaning land (*ayi*) sacred (*zan*). This Lwa rules the markets, denoting her power to handle all sorts of transactions between the worlds of the living and the dead.

Ayizan's Veve

Her characteristic symbol is the imperial palm, which reflects integrity and justice, while its leaf, when still closed, symbolizes purity. About this Lwa, Frater Vameri says:

> Ayizan, besides being at the head of the Mambos' craft, is also a Lwa that operates in the market (the importance of the mar-

ket for some African people would yield a separate text) and is also related to the forest and plants. So, her protections and cures, of course, will have some use of natural knowledge. Here we see the clear theme of the close connection between the priesthood and Gran Bwa, the Lwa of the forest. The forest, of course, is a place of mystery by nature, which points to the undoubted magical nature of the priesthood in Vodou. In this context, we must remember that Gran Bwa is one of the masters of Vodou magic. Consequently, Loko and Ayizan share this magical power.[44]

Ayizan is associated with the lithograph of Jesus being baptized by John the Baptist and Saint Anne. Her number is seven and her colors are white and silver. She drinks beer or *trempe*, an alcoholic beverage made from raw sugarcane seasoned with medicinal and aromatic herbs. She also smokes a pipe, and her ceremonies are usually secret.

Damballah

Also known as Damballah Wedo, the creator serpent from the great serpent god of the Fon, symbolized by the rainbow and called Dan. This serpent envelops the entire world, bringing his tail into his mouth, symbolizing

---

44. Vameri, "Loko e Ayizan."

unity and wholeness, and expressing his function as the ordainer of the entire cosmos.

Damballah's Veve

In Africa, two beings are seen as a single entity: Da or Dan, the serpent of the earth, and Ayida, the rainbow serpent. Precisely because he is a union between these two deities, which are seen as complementary and integral to a whole, another name of this Lwa is Dan-Ayida Wedo. His attributes are wisdom, fecundity, abundance, fertility, and rain. The saint associated with Damballah is Saint Patrick, as is Moses, given the connection of both with serpents.

Damballah is served with white utensils, and his altars are covered in white satin with a crucifix on top. He is offered white chickens, white eggs, white rice, milk, an egg over a pile of white flour, white wine, rice pudding, white grapes, coconut, champagne, and Anisette. In some homes, no alcoholic beverages are offered to Damballah, as it is believed that he does not appreciate the odor of alcohol or tobacco.

Agwé

Agwé is the sailor of the seas, the lord of the oceans. He patronizes fishermen, sailors, and everyone who earns a living at sea or from the sea. He is the lord of shipwrecks and the treasures they hide. Agwé commands the winds that blow in the oceans, the marine hurricanes, and the tsunamis. His domain also extends to intuition, deep emotions, and psychic abilities.

His depiction is that of a Black man with green eyes, and his colors are white and navy blue. He is the husband of La Sirene, the mermaid. A myriad of spirits connected to the seas serve him.

Agwé's Veve

The saint associated with him is Saint Ulric, and his parties are always held on the beach, serving sweets and cakes on white towels and white porcelain. His drinks are champagne, white wine, and coffee, always accompanied by the finest *petit fours*.

La Sirene/La Balen

La Sirene or Lasiren ("the mermaid") and La Balen ("the whale") are the sisters of the seas. La Sirene is a beautiful woman with black hair and a fish tail, a classic representation of the mythical mermaid. She is feminine, charming, and sensual. Like the Orisha Yemaya, she is called the mother of fish, but she does not carry the maternal attributes of this Yoruba goddess, and her striking characteristics are seduction and charm. She does not eat any live animals and rarely takes any food, although some houses honor her with delicate *pâtisserie*. Her favorite offerings are champagne, perfume, and toiletries.

As Frater Vameri cautions, "The maritime quality of La Sirene borrows the unpredictability of the tides," so she can be "welcoming like the calm sea," but she can also be "relentless like sea storms."[45]

---

45. Vameri, "A Sereia das Antilhas."

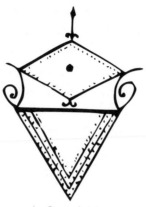

La Sirene's Veve

La Sirene's counterpart is La Balen, her Black sister, who is profoundly intuitive and swims in the dark depths of the ocean, not in the clear waters in which the Mermaid reigns. When they manifest through possession, La Sirene always gets on the floor, where she begins to chant her melodious and hypnotic song. In contrast, La Balen, also on the floor, begins to cry and make sounds reminiscent of whales.

Erzulie Freda

Erzulie or Ezili is a family of Lwas or spirits. The great M found in almost all their veves is the first letter of *Maîtresse*, "mistress" in French.

Erzulie Freda, or simply Ezili, is a highly magical and beautiful deity whose full name is really Maîtresse Mambo

Erzulie Freda Dahomey. All these words refer to various aspects of this beautiful Lwa, who is one of the best known, most loved, and also most difficult to understand deities of the Vodou pantheon. She is at the same time powerful and benevolent but also terrible and highly demanding.

Erzulie Freda reigns over romantic love, luxury, luck, abundance, refinement, and everything related to the world of riches and power. She also governs dreams, hopes, and aspirations. More than simply being the expression of love, Erzulie Freda is the very symbol of the perfection of the universe. She is associated with freshness, cleanliness, and purity so that, in her presence, no poison, maleficent magic, or curse can prosper.

Erzulie Freda's Veve

Erzulie Freda is known as the lover because she acts more like one than a wife, although she is married to several Lwas and is very fond of marrying her devotees. She is known to have three Lwas as husbands: Ogou Feray, Damballah, and Met Agwé Tawoyo. She wears three wedding rings, one for each husband. When she rides a devotee through possession, she flirts with all men and treats all women as rivals.

Erzulie Freda Dahomey is the Rada aspect of Erzulie. Gay men receive special protection from her. Her symbol is a heart; her colors are pink, light blue, white, and gold; and her offerings include daggers, jewelry, strong cigarettes, perfumes, sweet pies, dark cream, fine *pâtisserie*, wine, rum, champagne, red roses, paintings with a mother and a son, or her veve. Her offerings are arranged on the finest porcelain and in the most delicate crystal glasses and goblets. Her favorite perfume is *Anais Anais*, but she also accepts *Loção Pompeia* (Pompeia lotion), traditionally used in Vodou, and rose water. She has a lot of class and loves beauty and elegance.

Erzulie Freda is the representation of femininity and compassion. However, she also has a dark side, as she is seen as jealous and spoiled in some Vodou circles. In general, the French manners and capricious personality of Erzulie refer to the white French women who lived in Port Prince during colonization. In other words, the image of Erzulie that was gradually built in the popular imagination reflected the way enslaved Haitians saw the French who inhabited the cities of Haiti.

In Christian iconography, she is usually associated with the *Mater Dolorosa* of Jerusalem, given the traditional iconography in which Mary appears surrounded by jewels. She is never able to attain the most fervent desire of her heart. For this reason, her work always ends in tears because, in her eyes, nothing is ever perfect enough.

About the tears of Erzulie Freda, Frater Vameri makes beautiful considerations:

> Freda cries. This is a fact. The reason is subject to speculation, but as already mentioned, the most frequent understandings point to dissatisfaction. However, if she is the feminine expressing love to achieve balance, she cries because the task is arduous. She cries for the women whose role in the world is central and who are so underestimated. She cries for the men who fail to understand how beautiful, strong, and indispensable feminine nature is. She cries because we are all here, on this earth, without ever being able to reach the state of perfection. She cries because without perfection, we cannot truly unite with her. She cries because she still hasn't achieved her goal. It is indeed dissatisfaction, but it is not empty. The question is: why don't we cry with her? [46]

---

46. Vameri, "Erzulie Freda."

Cousin Zaka

Cousin Zaka (Uncle Zaka) is a farmer who comes from the traditions of the Taino people. Tradition says he was the first Lwa to talk to the natives residing on the island of Haiti. Given Haiti's agricultural economy, Zaka is one of the most popular Lwas, associated with Saint Isidore. He dresses like the peasants and wears a wide hat to protect himself from the sun. He always carries a bag with him, where he keeps his pipe, tobacco, a coconut, brown sugar, and some money.

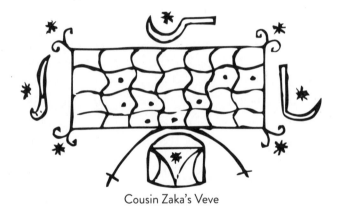

Cousin Zaka's Veve

Assuming the typical peasant's profile, he distrusts the townspeople, for he does not know how to read or write and fears being deceived by literate men. Because he is very jealous of his possessions, Vodouists often ask him to take care of their belongings.

It is customary to ask Zaka for money when on land, as it is believed that this money will bring luck to its possessor. However, Zaka will charge this loan with high interest the next time he manifests, and it is commonly said that for each currency unit borrowed from Zaka, he will require ten others.

Ogou

Lwa of the Nago or Yoruba nation, Ogou has the same characteristics as the known Orisha Ogun. He is the lord of iron and battles, remarkable in his honesty and righteousness, strength, and "hot" temperament. His color is red and he carries a machete, the typical Haitian machete. There are several Ogous, such as Ogou Balindjo, who walks with Agwé; Ogou San Jak, who poses as a crusader; and Ogou Badagris, who is a skilled political general. Other Orishas of the Yoruba pantheon are also hailed as Ogou, as Ogou Batala (Obatalá), and Ogou Shango (*Xangô*). National heroes are also worshipped as Ogou Dessalines, the divinization of Jean-Jacques Dessalines. There are many different aspects of the Lwa, just as there are many aspects of each of us.

Surprisingly, water is also associated with this Lwa, as Frater Vameri observes:

> Milo Rigaud states in his book on Veves that the Ogou are spirits of fire and water.

This combination may seem strange. However, he agrees with what has already been said. Let's remember that it is water (or oil, but a liquid) that tempers the iron in the forge. Without this watery element, tools and weapons do not reach their sweet spot. Therefore, it is not surprising that the Ogou also have water qualities.[47]

Ogou's Veve

Ogou drinks rum and smokes cigars. In the Rada pantheon, he is syncretized with Saint James the Great, while in the Petro pantheon, Ogou Feray is syncretized with Saint George.

---

47. Vameri, "Um pouco sobre Ogou."

Petro

Here are some of the Petro Lwas.

Met Kalfou or Maître Carrefour

After comparing the veve of Papa Legba and of Kalfou, who is seen as a Petro manifestation of this Lwa, one can conclude the significant difference between the two: while the veve of Papa Legba is symmetrical, symbolizing the cosmic order and method in its actions, Kalfou's is asymmetrical, showing two crossed serpents, in an allusion to the fact that he rules the chaos that underlies universal order. He is the guardian of the threshold, the lord of the forbidden and unknown realms. Cemeteries, death, and destructive magic are associated with him.

Met Kalfou (Maître Carrefour)'s Veve

Unlike Papa Legba who, when possessing a devotee, presents himself as an old man who limps, Kalfou manifests himself as a brave warrior and often eats embers and handles incandescent metal objects. He is a strong and aggressive spirit, quick to meet the requests addressed to him, but also very quick to punish, which is why when you go to him, you need to be careful and have the utmost respect. His colors are black and red, and he enjoys tobacco and strong alcoholic beverages seasoned with pepper.

Kalfou is intricately linked to Haiti's feared secret societies and is usually served only by adequately trained Houngans and Mambos. Yet, due to his terrible and dark appearance, Kalfou is also worshipped by the *bokors*, the sorcerers who live on the margins of Vodou society. Drawing a parallel with Yoruba tradition and with Brazilian Kimbanda, it can be considered that Kalfou reflects the vengeful aspect of the Orisha Eshu, as well as the aggressive and terrible aspects of the popular conception of the "chaotic" spirits of Kimbanda. This correlation is corroborated by the fact that the saint associated with Kalfou is Saint Anthony of Padua, also syncretized with Eshu in some strands of Umbanda and Kimbanda.

Erzulie Dantor or Ezili Danto

Ezili or Erzulie Dantor (also written *Dantò* or *Danthor*) is the Petro aspect of the Lwa Erzulie family. Like her sister Freda, Erzulie Dantor is extremely popular in Haiti, although she is equally feared. While Erzulie Freda is the typical white, French city woman from the time of colonization, Erzulie Dantor is Black and a countrywoman. She is a mother who is always working for her children and who goes to great lengths to protect them, but who is also overly aggressive and vindictive. She is considered the mother of the Petro nation and unlike Freda—who always breaks down in tears when confronted with harsh reality—Dantor usually expresses her anger by showing her fists, clenching her teeth, and babbling "Ke, ke, ke, ke." (Some songs allude to the fact that her tongue has been cut out, a common punishment in times of slavery.)

Erzulie Dantor is considered the Lwa of single mothers in particular. Her colors are red and blue, and her altars are usually covered with red towels and decorated with red carnations. She is always seen wearing the blue denim dress typical of Haitian peasant women. Precisely because of this, it is quite common to put a Black doll with a blue dress on her altars.

Dantor's love for knives is expressed in her veve, which always has a sword through a heart, as well as in the custom of offering knives to those possessed by her at ceremonies. When she *monta seu cavalo* ("rides her horse"), Dantor likes to do activities in favor of her initiates, who she takes as her children. Thus, it is quite common to see Dantor cleaning sacrificed animals and cooking them for the audience while the other Lwas interact with those present. Showing her care for her children, she washes their hands and faces and then serves them food. She is married to three powerful Petro Lwas: Ogou Feray, Ti-Jean Petro, and Simbi Makaya. Ogou Feray taught her the magic of forging metals and woods, Ti-Jean Petro transmitted his many magical formulas, and Simbi Makaya passed her knowledge about medicines and poisons. Regarding her first husband, the fact that he is also married to Freda is one of the reasons for the rivalry between the two sisters.

Erzulie Dantor (Ezili Danto)'s Veve

The saint associated with her is the Black Madonna of Częstochowa, Poland, precisely because of the scars she bears on her face, resulting from an attack on the original image in 1430. Copies of the icon of the Black Madonna of Częstochowa are believed to have been brought to

Haiti by Polish soldiers fighting on both sides of the Haitian Revolution from 1802 onward. Some say these scars are similar to those Dantor carries as memories of her fights with Freda, while others see a link between these scars and the traditional facial cuts (scarification) of some African ethnic groups. Other depictions of Erzulie Dantor include the Black Madonna, as well as Our Lady of Lourdes and Our Lady of Mount Carmel.

Tradition has it that the first demonstration of Erzulie Dantor took place at the ceremony held in *Bwa Kayiman*, which started the Haitian revolution. On this occasion, Erzulie Dantor would have possessed Mambo Cecile Fatiman and received, through her, the sacrifice of a black sow, a custom that continues to this day. She is also offered *griot*, a Haitian dish made from pork that is very spicy. Dantor drinks *kleren* (also known as clairin, a type of rum from Haiti), cocoa liquor, and unsweetened coffee. She smokes any strong and unfiltered cigarette and is very fond of Florida Water, a traditional cologne of widespread use in Vodou and Caribbean practices.

Simbi

Since Freda is associated with the rivers and La Sirene and Agwé rule the seas, Simbi reigns over the brackish waters of the marshes. For this reason, the name of one of his main manifestations is Simbi Andezo, a word originating from the French *dans deux eaux*, "in two waters." Unlike Damballah, a giant python snake, Simbi is seen as a small, fast water snake. Unlike the other Petro spirits, who are seen as fierce and aggressive, Simbi is shy and withdrawn, although his possession is sometimes violent. Simbi is constantly summoned to act in magical works, particularly for protection.

As with other Lwas, Simbi is the name of a family that has various manifestations, in total more than twenty. Among the best known are Simbi Andezo, associated with the marshes, as already seen; Simbi Makaya, a sorcerer directly linked to Haitian secret societies, particularly the Zobop and the Sanpwel; Simbi Ganga, a courageous warrior; Simbi Dlo, connected to rainwater and springs; and Simbi Anpaka, a specialist in herbs and leaves. A very curious modern association that some Houngans and Mambos have been making with Simbi is considering him a patron of electronic equipment, especially computers.

Simbi is a mysterious Lwa associated with magic, secrecy, and Haitian secret societies. There are several theories about his origin, with some arguing that he is one of the ancestral spirits worshipped by the Taino people, while others maintain that he came from Africa, more particularly from the Kongo and its *bisimbi* spirits, intermediaries between the deities and the dead. In a more esoteric view of this Lwa, he is the Vodou equivalent of Mercury, shepherding us from the material to the ethereal domain, which connect at the crossroads. The Vodou Mercury takes on the name of Simbi, a complex Lwa who embraces the task of guiding departed souls using the four directions of the cross. He is the emissary of Legba and the Sun's herald.[48]

Simbi's Veve

The colors associated with Simbi vary from temple to temple; they may be red and green or red and black. The saint associated with him is Saint Andrew. It is customary to offer him a turtle, whose blood is used by Simbi to make a potion against poisons and maleficent magic. As an effective healer, Simbi is also sought after by the sick and those who seek the healing properties of herbs.

Gran Bwa

Intricately linked to Papa Loko, Gran Bwa (from the French *gros bois*, "large wood") is an extremely popular Lwa,

48. Rigaud, *Secrets of Voodoo*.

as he is associated with the *demambwe*, the native forests of the island, and their many powers, secrets, and terrors. Since it is possible to find both sustenance and death in the woods, Gran Bwa knows all the secrets of plant remedies and poisons as well. He is also associated with the Mapou tree (*Cyphostemma mappia*), the symbolic tree of Vodou, considered the point of union between the kingdom of the living and the dead, so much so that the central mast (*poteau-mitan*) in every Vodou temple represents this tree.

It is said that in 1791, François Mackandal made use of Gran Bwa's herbs and roots to prepare the poison with which he and his followers killed many white plantation owners. Like Simbi, Gran Bwa is also worshipped by feared secret societies, among them the *Bizango* and the *Sanpwel*, who turn to him to work with "zombie cucumber," better known as jimsonweed (*Datura stramonium*), a plant used in the preparation of zombification powder.

He is sometimes known as *Gran Bwa d'Ilé*, a reference to the mythical island that lies on the ocean floor and on which the dead would await their return to land or their definitive trip to *Ginen*. He is also the lord of *Vilocan*, the sacred sunken city of the Lwas.[49]

Gran Bwa is one of the softest Petro Lwas. His possessions are not usually violent, and when he arrives, he is always ready to transmit some of his knowledge, wisdom,

---

49. Vameri, "Gran Bwa."

and protection to those present. His colors are red and green, and his associated saint is Saint Sebastian. He likes rice, beans, or corn covered with honey and laid out on banana leaves, as well as spiced rum. Another custom associated with this Lwa is offering money to forest protection organizations on his behalf.

Gran Bwa's Veve

Some say that with Met Kalfou and Baron Cemitierè, Gran Bwa forms the triad of the three Vodou sorcerers. According to this vision—which ends up excluding Simbi as also a great magician, but which is still interesting—Gran Bwa represents the green lands and the dark forests of the road of life; Met Kalfou would be the road itself, with its many paths and crossroads; and the Baron Cemitierè would be the journey's end. In particular, Frater Vameri shares essential information about the magical aspects of this Lwa:

Because of his centrality as the holder of the mysteries of the leaves, Gran Bwa is one of the great "magicians" of Vodou. His strength is fundamental to the making of a *wanga* [a Vodou charm/spell]. His presence is indispensable in priesthood ceremonies. The leaves, of course, are indispensable for the ritualistic functioning and magical operations within Vodou. So, it is not hard to understand why this Lwa is a master of magic.

As it turns out, although not always remembered in the most popular literature on Vodou, Gran Bwa is the lord and guardian of profound mysteries, linked to mystical and mythical underwater locations and the magic that underpins Vodou itself.

Veves: The Lwa's Magic Signatures

Any graphic allusion to Vodou, whether in paintings, photographs, or movies, always brings mysterious symbols painted on walls and objects of worship, or drawn on the ground with corn flour. They are the famous veves (also spelled vèvè and vevè), symbols that, in addition to representing the Lwas themselves, are true beacons by which they guide themselves, when invoked, on their journey from *Ginen* to the world of the living.

Sometimes, veves are scratched with chalk or drawn with gunpowder or ash. The most common and traditional method of drawing them, however, is with corn flour, and only a priest or priestess can do it because it involves a priestly bestowal conferred in one of the secret rites of *kanzo*.

It is a mistake, however, to see them as mere symbolism: like the *zimbas* of Kimbanda, the veves create portals between worlds, calling the real presence of the Lwa and serving as the focal point where candles, drinks, and food are presented.

Milo Rigaud, who dedicated a whole work to the subject, asserts that these intricate ritual diagrams hold a captivating allure. They serve as pivotal junctures for cosmic energies, attracting planetary influences via enigmatic geometric patterns. Each veve assumes the role of a dynamic energy hub, exclusively harnessed by the discerning Houngan who possesses an intimate understanding of its intent and characteristics, allowing for its meticulous reproduction.[50]

In other words, in veves, the representation of astral force is distinct when compared to the approach used by the artisan crafting the *asson*. The process of fashioning the *asson* within the sacred *oum'phor* serves as a Vodou magical emulation of the actual astral forces, effectively reproducing their essence.

In Vodou rituals, the act of reconstructing the astral energies enshrined within the veves has the inherent ability to summon the Lwas (symbolic embodiments of celes-

---

50. Riguad, *Ve-Ve Diagrammes Rituels de Voudou.*

tial entities, stars, and planets) from their ethereal domains to the material realm. Although this might initially seem implausible, the undeniable authenticity of this occurrence becomes readily evident and tangibly experienced when observing a Vodou ceremony. Simply contemplating the intricate choreography of ritual components is enough to foster a sense of conviction.[51]

Nicholaj de Mattos Frisvold, in turn, notes that "the signatures of the spirits of the various Lwas are structured around the basic shape of the crossroads," where "we realize unity and move forward, to where miracles are made possible."[52] In fact, this seems to be a common mystery for the Afro-diasporic practices that make use of traced signs (and not only them): the crossroads, a source of power beyond space-time and not belonging to the world of the living nor the world of the dead, the ground on which human beings tread. And it is at this crossroads that, as we saw, the first Lwa to be called to open the gate that separates the worlds is Papa Legba.

As mentioned before, there is heated controversy about the origin of the veves—this seems to be a constant when the topic is Vodou. Thus, regarding the African, European, and American origins of veves, Yvonne Chireau and Mambo Vye Zo Komande LaMenfo state that veves

---

51. Rigaud, *Secrets of Voodoo*.
52. Frisvold, *A Arte dos Indomados*.

emerged as iconic visual emblems or coats of arms. With their roots embedded in the era of Haitian enslavement, veves trace their conceptual heritage back to the cultural and spiritual orientations of West and Central Africa, while also drawing inspiration from the diverse representations and visual traditions of indigenous practices in the Americas and Europe. Analogous to other artistic creations in the Vodou tradition, veves manifest organically, shaped by spontaneity, adaptation, and imagination. Veves were astutely characterized as "fragments of Africa," yet they also incorporate vestiges of the Taino people and the Enlightenment, interwoven with threads from Jesuit and Freemason legacies as well as other diverse origins.[53] Clearly, veves are a result of multiple influences.

So, where did the veves truly originate? Precisely in this fusion of cultures and knowledge, sewn with the needle of necessity.

---

53. Chireau and LaMenfo, "Esoteric Writing of Vodou."

CHAPTER 4
VOODOO IN
NEW ORLEANS

In Brazil, Vodou is still lesser known and associated with old prejudices. Generally, in Brazil, those who are not familiar with Vodou associate it with low-level spiritual practices such as little dolls stuck with pins, etc. They are also unaware that Vodou is one of the official religions of Benin and is practiced by approximately 12 percent of the population.[54] In the local language, Ewe, *Vodou* means "spirit."[55] Every year, at the beginning of January, several West African Vodou groups gather in the coastal town of Ouidah to demonstrate their religious practices and celebrate their beliefs.

Voodoo followers in the United States—which, for its differences from Haitian Vodou, we chose to spell

---

54. Office of International Religious Freedom, "2021 Report on International Religious Freedom."
55. "Vodou, Serving the Spirits."

Voodoo—continued to use images of Catholic saints for their spirits. As a result of the fusion of French culture and Voodoo in Louisiana, although Voodoo and Catholic practices are radically different, both saints and spirits act as mediators, such as the Virgin Mary and Legba, presiding over specific activities. However, it cannot be said that this process of associating saints with spirits was just syncretism, as American Voodoo actually absorbed the practice of saints as carried out by the Catholic Church.

Louisiana Voodoo

New Orleans has been declared the most haunted city in America. Tour guides have sought to invest in the legends of vampires, werewolves (*loup-garou*), and very traditional macabre stories in Louisiana. Voodoo fans have a less morbid relationship with death—therefore, the conventional images of skulls and skeletons. But for sure, the city's oldest and deepest hidden traditions involve the mysterious practices of Voodoo.

The city oozes Voodoo and Hoodoo in an open way, seemingly without prejudice. When one knows the real purpose of Voodoo, one realizes that it has nothing to do with the negative stereotypes and prejudices associated with the dark magic with which it is labeled. Like any city linked to religiosity, New Orleans is highly marketed, with several stores selling religious items and providing spiritual services.

Today, the main focus of Louisiana Voodoo is to serve others and influence the outcome of life events through connection with nature, spirits, and ancestors. Authentic rituals are performed "behind closed doors" because a showy ceremony would be considered disrespectful to the spirits. Voodoo methods include divination, spiritual baths, specially planned diets, prayer, and personal ceremonies. Voodoo is often used to cure anxiety, addiction, depression, loneliness, and other ailments. It seeks to help the hungry, the poor, and the sick, as Marie Laveau used to do.

Voodoo Deities

Although American Voodoo is a derivation of Haitian Vodou, there are significant differences between the two. Of the many Lwas worshipped in Haiti, few reached the United States and were worshipped there. The main and best-known Vodou Lwa is Papa Legba, also known as Papa La-bas or Papa Limba. His attributes and functions are the same as the original Haitian Lwa, but there is a great emphasis on his role as guardian of the crossroads, the paths of the physical and spiritual worlds that intersect.

As in almost all religions of the Black diaspora, Papa Legba was associated with the devil, and many legends began to originate from there. Perhaps the strongest and most widespread belief about Papa Legba is that jazz and blues musicians who want to become experts in the art of playing their instrument and highly creative in musical composition should make a pact with Papa Legba at midnight, at a crossroads. The Faustian contours of this legend are evident, and the success achieved by big names in music from the Southern United States, such as Robert Johnson and Tommy Johnson, was attributed to a pact with "the old man at the crossroads." In 1986, the movie *Crossroads* premiered, a drama inspired by the legend of Robert Johnson and his pact with Papa Legba.

Another great devotion in Voodoo is the adoration of the Virgin Mary and, in particular, of Our Lady of Perpetual Help. Here it is important to note that this is not about syncretism but the service of the mother of Jesus herself. Although the New Orleans Voodoo recreation movement of the 1970s introduced the sect of Erzulie Freda, syncretized with Our Lady, the original followers did not know Erzulie.

Portrayed in fantasy films and novels, another very celebrated deity of Louisiana Voodoo is Li Gran Zombi, represented by a python present in the practice and with which the priestesses dance. The origin of this spirit is Nzambi, the creator god of the Kongo people. Li Gran Zombi is believed to have absorbed characteristics of

Damballah and Simbi, although he is an entirely distinct spiritual being.

American Voodooists commonly turn to Saint Michael to protect themselves from evil. However, they believe that the archangel responds more readily to those who invoke him by his secret name: Daniel Blanc, Danny, or Blanc Dani. According to some, the allusion to the color white derived from the absorption of attributes of Damballah by the Voodoo practice of Saint Michael.

Among the saints most invoked by American Voodooists are Saint Expeditus, Saint Judas (Jude) Thaddeus, and Saint Roch, considered able to provide miracles and wonders to their devotees. Also very popular are Saint Joseph, Assonquer, and John the Conqueror. Material requests are usually made to Saint Joseph, especially financial requests, as well as requests from men abandoned by their wives. Monetary and professional help is requested from Assonquer, a forgotten spirit in Africa itself, which is worshipped in the images of Saint Louis IX. As for John the Conqueror, local folklore says he was an African prince captured and enslaved in the southern US who became famous for his cunning. John the Conqueror lends his name to the most powerful root used in Voodoo oils and powders, the Jalapa root or *Ipomoea purga*.

Also popular are Joe Féraille, Saint Marron, and Yon Sue. Joe Féraille is an aspect of Ogou Feray considered a pirate and mercenary; he responds to the requests of his faithful through a lot of bargaining. Legend has it that Saint Marron was an enslaved man named Squire and was one of the most accomplished dancers of the Voodooist practices held in Congo Square. In the early nineteenth century, he tried to flee the property in which he lived and worked but was captured and his right arm was seriously injured. Due to an infection, his arm had to be amputated. After this incident, Squire escaped and became famous as the outlaw Bras-Coupé ("severed arm"), leader of a group of *marrons* ("Maroons"), enslaved fugitives like him. After his death, he began to be worshipped, and his help is sought after in cases involving persecution of any kind. As for Yon Sue, he is Saint Anthony of Padua, whose devotion was spread especially by Marie Laveau.

Also worth mentioning are the spirits of Indigenous people, which are very popular in the United States, where there are Spiritual churches that mix Pentecostalism, Voodoo, Catholicism, and lectures that incorporate spiritual guides. The most famous Indigenous spirits in Louisiana are Black Eagle, Black Hawk, and Yellow Jacket.

Voodoo Logistics

Contrary to some hasty or opportunistic mentions that have been seen lately, American Voodoo is as initiatory a practice as Haitian Vodou, relying on initiation ceremonies essential to the consecration of its priests and priestesses. The Voodoo Mambos and Houngans, therefore, also undergo rigorous preparation that involves theoretical-practical training, as well as reserved rites that give them priestly power and authority.

An example of this is the research carried out by photographer Shannon Taggart on a Brooklyn Mambo. Shannon Taggart, after photographing Spiritualists—people who believe they can communicate with the dead—in the state of New York, has documented Voodoo since moving to Brooklyn in 2005. Taggart's project began when she met a Mambo named Rose Marie Pierre, who ran a temple in the basement of a store in a working-class neighborhood. There, Taggart captured images of priests incorporating the Lwa.[56] Horne mentions that photographer Shannon Taggart was attracted to what she calls "psychological spaces." She describes them as "invisible realities, like an interior experience that you can't really see" and enjoys the challenge of creating images that capture them.[57]

---

56. Little, "Basement Vodou."
57. Horne, "Picturing the Invisible."

Voodoo in New Orleans distinguishes itself by making use of a series of magical resources from various cultures. Thus, priests and priestesses offer services such as tarot and crystal ball readings, herbal treatments, spells, amulets, and talismans. Among these practices, candle magic is distinguished, basically based on the symbolism associated with colors. There are two systems of symbolic attribution of candle colors, the first of which was shared by Zora Neale Hurston: [58]

- White: Peace and undoing spells (uncrossing)
- Red: Victory
- Pink: Love
- Green: Success
- Blue: Protection
- Yellow: Money
- Brown: Bring money and attract people
- Violet: Cause harm and triumph in a purpose
- Black: Malevolent magic

The second system derives from Henri Gamache, an author who was remarkably successful with *The Master Book of Candle Burning*: [59]

---

58. Lady Hannah, "The History of Candle Colour in Hoodoo."
59. Lady Hannah, "The History of Candle Colour in Hoodoo."

- White: Spiritual blessings and healing
- Red: Love and passion
- Pink: Attraction and romance
- Green: Money and good luck
- Blue: Peace and harmony
- Yellow: Money
- Brown: Judicial causes
- Violet: Cause harm and triumph in a purpose
- Purple: Control
- Orange: Opening of the paths
- Black: Repulsion and undoing of spells (uncrossing)
- Black and White: Return the evil to those who sent it
- Black and Red: Undoing love spells
- Green and Black: Undoing financial spells

Voodoo Destinations

An interesting tourist attraction of the city is the New Orleans Historic Voodoo Museum, located at 724 Dumaine Street, New Orleans, LA 70116-3140. Since 1972, the museum has been a permanent landmark and major tourist attraction in New Orleans, where you can learn about the rich culture that shapes this unique city and appreciate Voodoo's historical relics, paintings, sculptures, and other artifacts.

An important New Orleans temple is the Voodoo Spiritual Temple. It was founded in 1990 by Priestess Miriam Chamani and Priest Oswan Chamani. It is the only formally established Spiritual temple that focuses on traditional West African spiritual and herbal healing practices currently in existence in New Orleans. It is located at 1428 North Rampart Street, New Orleans, LA 70116. On March 6, 1995, Priest Oswan passed away, but Priestess Miriam continues to follow the tradition of the temple along with the spirit of Oswan. This temple expanded its spirituality around the world, including a temple in Russia.[60]

On February 1, 2016, an electrical fire broke out in the Voodoo Spiritual Temple. The temple suffered severe damage to its structure and contents. Although no one was injured, the incident left the Voodoo Spiritual Temple, which had been serving the community for twenty-six years, with an uncertain future.

Voodoo Dolls

When a layperson wants to know something about Voodoo, the first question they ask is usually about the dolls. Some people imagine Voodooists spend the entire day sticking needles into dolls, but this does not happen—dolls are just a detail of the religion. Of course, the dolls

---

60. See https://voodoospiritualtemple.org.

exist, work, and are used for various purposes, not only for revenge, which should be avoided as much as possible.

Some ancient civilizations, such as the Greeks, Egyptians, and Babylonians, used images and dolls for ceremonial use, and there are records of magical practices marginal to the official religion that involve the use of clay, wax, or wooden dolls. In the case of Voodoo, the object does not represent a god or a spiritual being.[61] It is used as an amulet to attract luck, money, employment, health, or love. There are many ways to make the doll, but the original, the preferred, is said to date back to Haitian Vodou (although there are no records of this practice in the most well-known Haitian traditions).

Voodoo dolls originated in the African diaspora as part of spiritual customs and today can be found in New Orleans Voodoo. It is uncertain whether Haitian magic influenced European magic or vice versa, as there are ancient records of dolls being used in European witchcraft. The doll often represents the person who wants to appeal to Voodoo spirits or the person who wants to be cured of some illness. In fact, the Voodoo doll can be very useful: we can work remotely on a sick person for healing, breaking spells, and much more. In addition, it is used in energizing processes, dismantling harmful magical work, spiritual

---

61. Sometimes, toy dolls are used to house a certain spirit or mystery.

cleansing, works of love, works of financial growth, and health cases.

There is a ritual to prepare the doll, from the choice and cleaning of the material to the songs. It is necessary to meditate on the desires, emotions, and feelings that one wants to put in the doll. The most practical way to dress the doll is to form a kind of soft fabric bag tied at the ends. Rustic fabric is more suitable, as it is more faithful to the traditions of origin. After the chanting, it is time to use the needles or pins, which are inserted to reinforce the request. In other words, contrary to popular belief, the presence of needles stuck in the doll does not necessarily involve an evil objective, as needles also serve as fluidic condensers in dolls aimed at noble purposes, such as health and prosperity. When the figure is ready, it is time to store it in a high, discreet place. Next to it, the faithful can place candles of the appropriate color and must pray every day to reinforce their request.

CHAPTER 5
MARIE LAVEAU: THE VOODOO QUEEN

What was so special about the woman who mobilized and fascinated New Orleans for many years? Sometimes considered the most powerful woman of her time, Marie Laveau is a figure shrouded in mystery who ended up becoming a myth in American history, particularly in New Orleans, where she was born on September 10, 1794,[62] in the French Quarter, *Vieux Carré*. Although there is not much reliable information, Marie Laveau, the Voodoo Queen, is part of the religious imagery of New Orleans. The great challenge for researchers has always been separating the real facts from the myths and legends that surround one of the greatest celebrities of the nineteenth century.

The first and main difficulty in researching her life and work is biographical data, which is generally incomplete.

---

62. Other sources list Marie Laveau's birth year as 1801.

Journalistic reporters and fiction authors produced a sensationalist description of New Orleans Voodoo and, consequently, of its queen, Marie Laveau. Some documents disappeared; others were falsified.

What we do know is that she was the illegitimate daughter of a respected politician, Charles Laveau Trudeau, and a free Black woman named Marguerite Henry. According to Fandrich, who wrote a dissertation on Marie Laveau, "Marie was baptized in St. Louis Cathedral in the French Quarter on September 16."[63] The event was inscribed in the sacramental register as a biracial child "born on the tenth day of this present month," the daughter of Marguerite and "an unknown father."[64]

Marguerite Henry was born in 1772 in New Orleans. She was freed by Henry Roche-Belaire in 1790 and lived a stable union, not legally recognized, with Henry D'Arcantel and began to use the name Marguerite D'Arcantel. Her relationship with Charles Laveau Trudeau resulted in the birth of Marie Laveau.

Charles Laveau, born in New Orleans in 1743, was one of the most influential military officers and politi-

---

63. Fandrich, *The Mysterious Voodoo Queen, Marie Laveaux.*
64. Fandrich, *The Mysterious Voodoo Queen, Marie Laveaux.*

cians in Spanish Louisiana.[65] Married to Charlotte Per-
rault, with whom he had four daughters, he was the sur-
veyor general of Spanish Louisiana for about twenty years
until his resignation in 1805. Charles was responsible for
the design of Lafayette Square of New Orleans, created
in 1788 as "Place Publique."[66] His name on maps and the
land grant is recorded as Don Carlos Trudeau.[67]

After the purchase of Louisiana,[68] Charles also served
as a recorder for the city of New Orleans and was president of the city council. During his tenure as a recorder,
Mayor James Mather resigned, and Charles Trudeau took
office on an interim basis for almost six months in 1812.
He died in 1816 and was buried at Saint Louis Cemetery
No. 1 in New Orleans.

Life Before Becoming the Queen of Voodoo

Widely portrayed in film and fine art, one of Marie's
best-known and most commonly accepted images dates

---

65. Some sources state Charles Laveau was a successful biracial
businessman.

66. "History of Lafayette Square."

67. Toledano, *The National Trust Guide to New Orleans*.

68. The French claimed the territory of *La Louisiane* (named after
King Louis XIV) in 1682. In 1762, France ceded the territory to
Spain, and it became official in 1763. Spain governed the colony
of Louisiana from 1763 to 1803. It was briefly sold back to the
French before being purchased by the United States.

back to 1920, made by painter Frank Schneider; it was based on an older painting by George Catlin, now lost. Marie Laveau was described as a tall, beautiful woman with black hair, dark reddish skin, and piercing eyes. She liked to wear colorful scarves on her head and big, shiny gold earrings. Her mother and grandmother, Marguerite and Catherine Henry, were Voodoo priestesses, a profession Marie learned in her teens. They were beautiful Black women, and Marie inherited this beauty to the extreme.

Marie's *Encyclopaedia Britannica* entry mentions that she was the granddaughter of a priestess in Saint-Domingue, modern-day Haiti. African spirituality was a part of her family. Marie was drawn to religion after her mother's passing, and she began to study under Dr. John Bayou, "a well-known Senegalese conjurer (root worker)."[69] It wasn't long before Marie had acquired status in New Orleans society and the Voodoo community.

In August of 1819, Marie married in the Saint Louis Cathedral of New Orleans. She wed a carpenter named Jacques Santiago Paris, a free Black man who was part of a large immigration to New Orleans in 1809, after the Haitian Revolution of 1804. The ceremony was conducted by Antoino de Sedella, better known as Père Antoine. Étienne Mazureau, who had a distinguished

---

69. *Encyclopaedia Britannica Online*, s. v. "Marie Laveau," by Shantrelle P. Lewis, updated September 29, 2023, https://www.britannica .com/biography/Marie-Laveau.

career as a lawyer in France and later in Louisiana, three-time attorney general and secretary of state, attended the ceremony as a witness.

The marriage certificate was filed at the Saint Louis Cathedral. It is said that Charles Laveau went to the registry office with his daughter to sign her marriage contract and bestow a dowry: he extended an *inter vivos* gift to the betrothed couple, transferring the rights to a half lot he owned. The lot was nestled within the Faubourg Marigny, the very soil that was once the Marigny plantation.[70] This neighborhood is east of the vibrant French Quarter.

The couple had two daughters: Felicité, born in 1817, and Marie Angèlie, born in 1822. It is not known for certain, but it is assumed that they died at a young age. Between March 1822 and November 1824, Jacques disappeared (or died) under mysterious circumstances. Some sources said that Marie got rid of him through Voodoo magic because he was abusive and deceitful; other sources said that Jacques abandoned her. The fact is that his body was not found, and no charges were filed against Marie. Thus, everyone assumed that he had died. From then on, Marie adopted the marital status of widow.

With no husband and few resources, Marie got a job as a hairdresser. Another version is that she set up a hair salon with the inheritance left by Jacques Paris. This work

---

70. Fandrich, *The Mysterious Voodoo Queen, Marie Laveaux*.

allowed her to have contact with the women of New Orleans society, making it possible for her to learn about everything that happened in her clients' lives, as the elite ladies often talked about their most intimate relationships. Occasionally, she served clients in their own homes. Marie's own house was always full of clients, Black and white, and her mind-reading skills were fantastic. Clients used to confess their secrets and fears to Marie, their lovers, their spouses' lovers, their financial situation, properties, family problems, business affairs, etc. They spoke and Marie listened attentively, as if she were a psychologist.

In Eliza Potter's book *A Hairdresser's Experience in High Life*, she shares a beautiful quote by Marie Laveau. We have paraphrased it here: Marie's profession often led her to the upper echelon of society, where a multitude of suffering existed in all its diversity, mirroring the world's vast array of troubles. Within these privileged circles, the hairdresser was an enduring confidante. The hairdresser's presence was woven seamlessly into conversations, entrusted with the most personal revelations. There were instances when Marie longed to withdraw from conversations intended to be private, yet she found herself serving the role of a silent listener. Voicing her desire to interrupt these discussions wasn't appropriate; thus, more often than not, she unintentionally bore the weight of undisclosed secrets.[71]

---

71. Potter, *A Hairdresser's Experience in High Life*.

It is likely that Marie's professional work as a hair-dresser was accompanied by religious work. She read the future using cards and did works to help people obtain large sums of money; an unofficial version says that she got her data through people who came to consult her as a Voodoo and Hoodoo practitioner. Consolidating herself as a healer, Marie left her formal job to dedicate herself to her skills as a Voodoo Priestess.

In 1825 Marie began a relationship with a white man, a descendant of French nobles, named (Louis) Christophe Dominick Duminy de Glapion, a veteran of the Battle of New Orleans, with whom she lived until his death in 1855. In 1831 the family resided in the French Quarter, on Saint Ann Street, between Rampart and Burgundy streets. Some say this residence was built around 1798 by Marie's grandmother, Catherine Henry. With Christophe, Marie had several children, but only two daughters, Marie Heloise Euchariste Glapion (born in 1827)[72] and Marie Philomène Glapion (born in 1836), reached adulthood. (Marie Philomène became Marie Laveau's successor, becoming known as Marie Laveau II, as we will see later.)

---

72. Carolyn Morrow Long mentions that Marie and Christophe's eldest daughter, Marie Heloise Euchariste Glapion, died in early 1862 and left three young children: Adelai Aldina, Marie Marguerite Onesta, and Victor Pierre Crocker, all raised by Pierre Crocker. Crocker died in 1857, and the orphaned children were raised in the family home by their grandmother, Marie Laveau.

Within the vibrant mosaic of New Orleans, a city bustling with a diverse population that included free Black citizens, almost every resident owned slaves—Marie Laveau included. Between 1828 to 1854, Marie and Christophe purchased and then sold eight enslaved individuals. Interestingly, some researchers argue that Marie Laveau and Christophe Glapion bought enslaved people to free them.[73]

Much like his contemporaries, Christophe ventured into the realm of financial speculation, dabbling in stocks, loans, and real estate ventures. Despite his business skills, Christophe became entangled in a web of debt as the 1840s drew to a close. Succumbing to the mounting pressure exerted by the Citizens Bank of Louisiana, Christophe sold two enslaved individuals to a friend of the family, Philippe Ross, in 1850.[74]

Life as the Voodoo Queen

Marie Laveau created her own form of Voodoo in New Orleans, where she practiced and taught her magical works. She was in high demand to perform gris-gris[75] and love spells; resolve social issues, business, curses, and

---

73. Ward, *Voodoo Queen*.

74. Long, *Spiritual Merchants*.

75. The gris-gris themselves are not important, but rather the intention that is put into them. A person who made gris-gris asked the Spirits for special powers.

fights with enemies; and grant prosperity. White judges and politicians even paid her over $1,000 (a lot of money at the time, and about $30,000 in 2023) to win elections.

Marie became close friends with the head priest of the Catholic Church of New Orleans, Père Antoine, who carried out social work with prisoners, considered the scum of society. Marie was his partner in this work. For her, Catholicism and Voodoo were different—but not conflicting—ways of serving the spiritual forces that governed the world. She used holy water, incense, images of saints, and Christian prayers and incorporated them into her Voodoo and Hoodoo rituals.

In 1724, the French instituted the Code Noir ("Black Code") in the Louisiana Territory, which granted enslaved people the ability to observe Sunday as a "day of rest and leisure." Although Code Noir was instituted in 1724, no laws were regulating the right of enslaved people to assemble. In 1817 the mayor of New Orleans, Augustin François de McCarthy, issued a city ordinance that restricted the congregation of enslaved people to a peripheral region of the city. This open area on the outskirts of the city, on Rampart Street, became known as Congo Square. There, enslaved people used Sunday to gather. These meetings consisted of singing, dancing, and religious ceremonies, including the Voodoo dance.

The types of Voodoo ceremonies held in Congo Square were quite different from traditional Voodoo. The authentic rituals of Voodoo were secret and aimed at the religious and ritualistic aspects, while Voodoo in Congo Square was predominantly a form of leisure and celebration of African culture. In the 1830s, Marie Laveau led Voodoo dances in Congo Square and performed darker, more secretive rituals on the shores of Lake Pontchartrain and Bayou Saint John. It is said that Marie Laveau predominantly led rituals in three central locations: her home on Saint Ann Street, Lake Pontchartrain, and Congo Square.

Before Marie Laveau was declared the Voodoo Queen of New Orleans, there were rivalries over who should rule the Voodoo community. Two women served as queen before her: Sanité Dédé reigned for several years before being usurped by Marie Saloppé. Marie Saloppé was one of Marie Laveau's teachers—she introduced Marie Laveau to the complexities of the religion and served as a guiding influence.

Marie Laveau's reign as Voodoo Queen was unchallenged until 1850, when a woman named Rosalie challenged her reign. To incite fear and awe, Rosalie placed a life-size wooden doll in her backyard. The doll was imported from Africa and was said to be a source of powerful magic; it was decorated with detailed carvings and beads. When Voodooists began to respect and admire

Rosalie because of the doll, Marie stole the statue. She was brought to court by Rosalie, but Marie used her powers of persuasion and influence to have the doll permanently removed.[76]

The Home of Marie Laveau

On Saint Ann Street, Marie's home not only embraced the entire Laveau-Glapion clan but also served as her sanctuary. It is said that she had multiple altars adorned with an abundance of candles, icons of revered saints, beautiful flowers, fresh fruits, and an array of other offerings. Every Friday, Marie's home became the setting for her weekly congregation, where she presided over an assembly of her closest followers. The soundscape was enriched by a choir, who sang along to the melodies orchestrated by an accordionist. Every attendee arrived dressed in white, adhering to a shared dress code that fostered a sense of unity. A white cloth was spread across the floor and covered with herbs, candles, coins, food, and liquor, an embodiment of the practice known as "spreading a feast for the spirits."[77]

---

76. *Encyclopaedia Britannica Online*, s. v. "Marie Laveau," by Shantrelle P. Lewis, updated September 29, 2023, https://www.britannica.com/biography/Marie-Laveau.

77. Long, *A New Orleans Voudou Priestess*.

Religious services began with Catholic prayers, such as the Hail Mary and the Our Father. Marie poured water or wine on the ground, saluting the four cardinal points, and struck the ground three times: "In the name of the Father, the Son, and the Holy Spirit." Then the participants sang and danced. These rituals were intended to invoke spirits to incorporate into the bodies of the faithful and give advice to the congregation. A shared meal accompanied the service.

In the backyard of her home, Marie Laveau also performed ceremonies that conjured the spirit of the Great Zombie, the deity Damballah Wedo, who, according to some accounts, manifested through a snake called Zombie; some say this snake was a gift from the Duke of Orleans. It is also said that Marie had a black cat and a black rooster.

During the 1930s, the Louisiana branch of the Federal Writers' Project conducted interviews with elderly residents of New Orleans. Some of the interviewees shared memories intimately linked to Marie Laveau. One interviewee shared a vibrant portrayal of an altar located in Marie's living room. The altar was a meticulously curated space dedicated to the creation of auspicious talismans, amulets, and charms, some bearing the imprint of marital blessings, while others remained unnamed and shrouded in mystery. Notably, effigies of Saint Peter and

Saint Marron were present on this altar, symbolic sentinels with profound spiritual essence.[78]

The People Marie Laveau Served

Marie formed a following among enslaved and free Black people, as well as upper-class white people and visitors to the city, who were welcome at her ceremonies. According to one scholar, the number of white attendees at Marie's weekly congregation surpassed the number of Black attendees.[79]

A regal chair, reminiscent of the bishop's seat within a traditional church, took center stage as Marie's throne, and it was there that she sat at the beginning of these gatherings. Marie cultivated an environment where attendees were encouraged to vocalize their aspirations and longings. The ambiance underwent a captivating metamorphosis as participants playfully encountered a mist of rum, paving the way for spirited dance. These gatherings lasted for seven to nine hours, and food and drink were shared as the event drew to a close.

Marie Laveau also provided nursing care, which included minor surgeries, and collected patients to be treated in her own home. Regardless of whether it was day, night, or bad weather, anyone was welcome at any

---

78. Long, *A New Orleans Voudou Priestess*.

79. Long, *A New Orleans Voudou Priestess*.

time, and they were fed and housed. In addition to practicing charity, Marie was also very pious, and for her, it was a pleasant task to strengthen fidelity to the church. Sometimes priests turned to Marie when attendance decreased at church; she generally recommended adding ammonia, sugar, and nutmeg to the water used to wash the church. In more serious situations, she advised pouring a bottle of whiskey in the four corners of the church. Reports from the time show that this practice increased attendance at liturgical services.

During outbreaks of yellow fever and cholera, Marie's presence was always requested to help care for the sick. In 1853, a committee of gentlemen, appointed at a mass meeting in the Globe Hall, asked Marie, on behalf of the people, for her collaboration in caring for those suffering from yellow fever. She gladly accepted the task and fought the epidemic where it was most intense. Because of her devotion, many escaped death. For Marie Laveau, it was an honor to work for the benefit of the sick.

Marie was known for her acts of charity and social action with the poor. She sponsored the education of an orphan at the Catholic Institute for Indigent Orphans and paid bail for some free Black women accused of minor crimes. As we discussed earlier, it was also her habit to visit prisoners with Père Antoine. To prisoners sentenced to death, she used to bring a serving of her famous gumbo recipe. It cannot be confirmed, but some reports say that at times, her food was poisoned to spare the prisoner from suffering a painful and degrading execution on the scaffold. Whenever a prisoner roused feelings of pity and compassion in her, Marie fought intensely to grant them pardon, or at least to obtain a lighter sentence, something she usually achieved.

Tallant's Tales of Marie Laveau

Robert Tallant was one of Louisiana's best-known authors. Born in 1909 in New Orleans, he attended the city's local public schools. Before pursuing a literary career, he worked as a bank teller, a clerk, and an advertising copywriter. His friendship with Lyle Saxon led to his position as editor of the Louisiana branch of the Federal Writers' Project during the 1930s and 1940s. In this position, he co-authored the work *Gumbo Ya-Ya: A Collection of Louisiana Folk Tales* with Lyle Saxon and Edward Dreyer. Some of his famous works are *Voodoo in New Orleans*, *The Voodoo Queen*, and *Mardi-Gras…As It Was*. A book review on the Kirkus website about *The Voodoo Queen* says: "In the period of preparation for this novel based on [Marie Laveau's] life, [Tallant] has separated facts from legend, reminiscence from nostalgia, and told her story as he feels it might have been. It looks like a novel, not a biography."[80]

---

80. Anonymous, Review of *The Voodoo Queen*.

In his best-selling *Voodoo in New Orleans*, published in 1946, Tallant wrote about Marie Laveau as nonfiction, but the work contained distortions and half-truths. Adherents of the religion blame Tallant's works for spreading false narratives of Voodoo being evil and violent. For example, he wrote that Marie led orgies that included sacrificing babies in her Voodoo rituals. (In April 1957, the author was found dead in his home at the age of forty-seven, a decade after publishing the book. Was it Voodoo's response to the untruths about Marie Laveau's activities? The question remains.)

Though the authenticity of Tallant's work is debatable, he reported one of Marie Laveau's most notable achievements, which is said to have occurred in 1830. The saga unfurled when an esteemed young man was arrested. Accusations linked him to a crime, and there was compelling evidence of his alleged wrongdoing. The young man's father, who had an unwavering determination to clear his son's name, sought help from Marie and promised her a generous reward in exchange for her assistance. On the day of reckoning, Marie embarked on a pre-dawn pilgrimage to Saint Louis Cathedral, where she knelt before the altar for hours. The entire time, she held three Guinea peppers in her mouth.[81] Then, she stealthily made her way

---

81. This pepper burns terribly; for this reason, the quantity carried by Marie is highlighted.

into the courtroom, adeptly placing the trio of peppers underneath the judge's chair. Marvelously, the young man was cleared of all charges, and his elated father expressed his gratitude by gifting Marie with a modest abode on Saint Ann Street, in close proximity to Congo Square.[82]

In fact, this was the house where Marie already lived. Legally, the house had belonged to her husband, Christophe, who died in the summer of 1855. After her husband's death, the family went through an intense financial crisis due to Christophe's reckless investments. The Saint Ann Street property was overtaken by debt, and Marie Laveau, her daughters, and her grandchildren were only able to continue living in the house thanks to the exonerated young man's father.

The End of Marie Laveau's Life

In the 1860s, Marie stopped practicing Voodoo in public due to poor health but was still seen around town working on social causes. According to some reports, she continued to practice Voodoo masterfully into her old age. She was bedridden in the final years of her life and was cared for by her youngest daughter Marie Philomène (Marie Laveau II).

By the 1870s, Marie had the delicate frailty of so many elders. On June 24, 1875, Marie was visited by a

---

82. Tallant, *The Voodoo Queen*.

correspondent from the esteemed New Orleans newspaper *The Picayune*. His descriptions of her portrayed a figure who was hunched over, burdened by physical frailty, though her complexion had a rich bronze undertone. Wisps of gray hair gracefully framed her face, and a cane provided steadiness for her trembling hand. In response to questions about her spiritual practices, Marie revealed that she no longer served Voodoo spirits and was committed to a "sacred faith."

Marie Laveau was a mystery and, for a long time, her story could not be separated from myth. She passed away on June 15, 1881, peacefully, in her bed. *The Picayune* published her obituary the following day:

Death of Marie Laveau

A woman with a wonderful history, almost a century old, carried to the tomb yesterday evening.

Those who have passed by the quaint old house on St. Ann, between Rampart and Burgundy streets, with the high, frail looking fence in front over which a tree or two is visible, have, till within the last few years, noticed through the open gateway a decrepit old lady with snow white hair, and a smile of peace and contentment lighting up her golden features. For a few years past she has been missed from her accustomed place. The feeble old lady lay upon her bed with her daughter and grandchildren around her ministering to her wants.

On Wednesday, the invalid sunk into this sleep which knows no waking. Those whom she had befriended crowded into the little room where she was exposed, in order to obtain a last look at the features, smiling even in death, of her who had been so kind to them.

At five o'clock yesterday evening, Marie Laveau was buried in her family tomb in St. Louis Cemetery No. 1. Her remains were followed to the grave by a large concourse of people, the most prominent and the most humble joining in paying their last respects to the dead. Father Mignot conducted the funeral services.[83]

In her obituary, *The Picayune* noted her pious nature and her devotion to Jesus:

All in all Marie Laveau was a most wonderful woman. Doing good for the sake of doing good alone, she obtained no reward,

---

83. For this and other quotes from Marie Laveau's obituary, see https://www.newspapers.com/article/the-times-picayune-marie -laveau-obit-188/24397240.

oft times meeting with prejudice and loathing, she was nevertheless contented and did not flag in her work. She always had the cause of the people at heart, and was with them in all things. During the late rebellion she proved her loyalty to the South at every opportunity and freely dispensed help to those who suffered in defense of the "lost cause." Her last days were spent surrounded by sacred pictures and other evidences of religion, and she died with a firm trust in heaven. While God's sunshine plays around the little tomb where her remains are buried, by the side of her second husband, and her sons and daughters, Marie Laveau's name will not be forgotten in New Orleans.

Still in the obituary:

A few years ago, before she lost control of her memory, she was rich in interesting reminiscences of the early history of this city. She spoke often of the young American Governor Claiborne....[84] She spoke sometimes of the strange little man with

---

84. William Charles Cole Claiborne was an American politician, the first governor of Louisiana. He was also said to be the youngest congressman in the history of the United States, being elected to the House of Representatives at the age of twenty-two.

the wonderful bright eyes, Aaron Burr,[85] who was so polite and dangerous. She loved to talk of Lafayette,[86] who visited New Orleans over half a century ago. The great Frenchman came to see her at her house, and kissed her on the forehead at parting.

The eminent writer Lafcadio Hearn referred to her as "one of the wonderful women who ever lived," and in Marie Laveau's 1881 obituary in *The New York Times*, he wrote:

Although Marie Laveau's history has been very much sought after, it has never been published.…The secrets of her life…could only be obtained from the old lady herself, but she would never tell the smallest part of what she knew.[87]

---

85. Aaron Burr Jr. was a United States military man and politician, the son of Aaron Burr. He was a lieutenant colonel in the Continental Army and a founding member of the Democratic-Republican Party in New York and strongly supported Governor George Clinton. He became the third vice president of the United States (March 4, 1801–March 4, 1805) during Thomas Jefferson's presidency.

86. Marie-Joseph Paul Yves Roch Gilbert du Motier, Marquis de La Fayette, known in the United States simply as Lafayette, was a French soldier who fought for the Patriots in the American War of Independence (Revolutionary War) and was an important figure in the French Revolution as well.

87. See https://bluestarowl.files.wordpress.com/2013/10/marie-laveau -obit.pdf for more.

Marie Laveau II

Marie's daughter, Marie Philomène, took care of the funeral arrangements for the evening of June 16, 1881, which was conducted in accordance with the dignified structure of the Catholic Church, without any demonstrations of Voodoo. According to some accounts of her death, she had departed from this life in an entirely Catholic atmosphere.

After Marie's death, New Orleans newspapers were full of stories about her holiness. Many people said that she continued to be seen in the city after that date. It was noted that her daughter, Marie Philomène, took her name (Marie Laveau II) and continued to practice magic after Marie's death, acquiring notoriety similar to that of her mother.

There was no shortage of people who said that the smiling old lady who lived in a room at the back of Marie Laveau II's house, who claimed to have been rescued from a life of poverty on the streets, was her own mother, Marie Laveau, who continued to teach her art to her daughter.

One researcher writes:

> [Marie's] death would be perfectly normal, except for the fact that it did not change the Voodoo meetings in Congo Square and Lake Pontchartrain, which she continued to conduct in the same way as always. That's

right—despite having a public burial with many witnesses, she remained serene and cheerful, as if nothing had happened...in fact, even too cheerful, as she didn't look even half her eighty-seven years old....She was alive and young. It seemed that the Voodoo Queen really had supernatural powers....The matter was only definitively resolved when Marie Laveau died again in 1897.[88]

There is no further evidence of when Marie Philomène took her mother's place and became Marie Laveau II. There appears to be no definitive date as to when the transition occurred, but it is likely that there was an eventual replacement first, followed by a complete takeover later. Like her mother, Marie Philomène was beautiful, and there was a remarkable physical resemblance between them. Marie Laveau II inherited and took up the art left by her mother and became known for her rituals in the marshes around New Orleans. Some are of the opinion that Marie Laveau II's celebrity has surpassed that of her own mother.

Marie Laveau II's spells became famous and continue to be practiced to this day. She made gris-gris for protection or prosperity that contained tiny pieces of bone, pebbles, graveyard dirt, salt, and red pepper. Once, she made

---

88. Note from the Authors: Here, the writer is referring to Marie Laveau II's death ("Pessoas Especiais: Marie Laveau").

a more elaborate gris-gris, considered a powerful weapon against evil, which contained the dry eye of a frog, a dry lizard, the little finger of a Black man who had committed suicide, the wings of a bat, the eyes of a cat, the liver of an owl, and the heart of a rooster. Phew!

Another prescription, ideal for luck in gambling, was to take a small piece of suede, another of red flannel, the tooth of a shark, the sap of a pine tree, and the blood of a pigeon. She mixed the blood with the sap and, with this mixture, wrote on the suede the amount the player intended to win. The suede was then covered with red flannel, the shark's tooth was placed between the pieces of material, and the pieces were sewn together with cat hair. The spell, once completed, should be placed inside the player's left shoe.

To get a "cheapskate" friend to spend all the money they had on a specific person (the client), Marie Laveau II instructed the client to take a bath in a bathtub with a small amount of borax, cinnamon, and a teaspoon of sugar. After the bath, the client would go directly to their stingy friend, and that friend would spend everything they had on the client.

Marie Laveau II's ways of performing herbal magic were incredible. Sick people were often brought to her to receive the blessing of a cure. Snake bites were common in that region; for this accident, she recommended capturing a live snake of any kind, cutting off its head while it struggled, and applying the head to the wound, leaving it tied there until sunrise the next day. She used traditional medicines in her treatments as well. She often used roots and herbs that had authentic therapeutic qualities. To alleviate swelling and discomfort, she used hot water with magnesium sulfate, rubbing the affected parts with whiskey while praying and lighting candles. She used to prescribe castor oil and other homemade medicines, always accompanied by prayers and candles.

Marie Laveau II learned the art of winning legal cases from her mother. To ensure a convict would be acquitted, she looked for the names of the jurors, the judge, and the prosecutor. She wrote the names on a piece of paper that was frozen inside an ice cube and then covered with sugar. She lit nine candles around the ice cube on the ground, fist clenched, reciting prayers in an unknown language. In the most difficult cases, she used an alternative: making the judge sick. She melted a black candle, put a piece of paper with the judge's name written on it inside the melted wax, made the wax into a ball, and placed it in a bathtub. The night before the trial, Marie Laveau II entered the tub and pushed the ball with a stick. The next day, the judge did not appear in court.

The most important man in the life of Marie Laveau II was not one of her many lovers. It was Dr. Jim, also called Indian Jim, who was three-quarters Native American and one-quarter Black. Initially, his reputation as a very competent Voodoo healer bothered Marie Laveau II, as her clientele were no longer consulting her and instead resorting to the powers of Dr. Jim, who used beer as one of his main tools to heal and ward off unwanted spirits. Marie Laveau II tried to report him to the police and threw gris-gris in his backyard, but her efforts to get him out of her way were futile. So, very intelligently, she decided to ally himself with him, teaching him her craft and learning healing techniques from him. It was often said that the spiritually troubled turned to Marie Laveau II, while the sick and injured sought the aid of Dr. Jim. He became very prosperous in New Orleans.

Marie Laveau II had a relationship with a white man, Emile Alexandre Legendre, who was thirteen years older than her and married. They had seven children between 1857 and 1870, all classified as biracial, and remained a couple until Emile died in 1872. After his death, Marie Laveau II returned to live with her mother, along with her seven children. Marie Laveau was in declining health and was cared for by Marie Philomène until her death.

There is not enough data to say how or when Marie Laveau II died and where she was buried. Some say she died in 1897. It is likely that she drowned during a violent storm at Lake Pontchartrain.

At the end of the nineteenth century, opinions about Marie Laveau II were divided. Some local journalists and popular writers praised her significant social action and exemplary benevolence, but others claimed that she took advantage of the superstitions of the naive. Even today, those who excel in spiritual practices are often labeled by many—with or without reason—as charlatans and profiteers of other people's good faith.

Marie Laveau's Legacy

Marie Laveau was well-liked and respected by many people who had benefited from her assistance or knew of her reputation for inclusiveness and charity. She also had her detractors, by whom she was feared, ridiculed, and stigmatized as a sorceress. Some newspapers from the time praised Marie Laveau, such as the New Orleans *Picayune*, but she also faced significant criticism. In 1859, a *Crescent* reporter was less kind—he called her "the notorious hag who reigns over the ignorant and superstitious as the Queen of the Voodoos."[89]

Marie Laveau's tomb in St. Louis Cemetery No. 1 is a landmark and tourist attraction in New Orleans. The crypt attracts many visitors, who often draw three crosses (XXX) on the side as a magical prayer, hoping that her spirit will grant them the fulfillment of one or more wishes. People still leave offerings, candles, flowers, and Voodoo dolls in the crypt. Some visitors claim to have seen the ghost of Marie Laveau inside the cemetery.

89. Filan, *The New Orleans Voodoo Handbook*.

Marie Laveau formulated the first doctrine for a Voodoo practice, and her reputation has been kept alive in songs, films, and novels. She was portrayed in the *American Horror Story* television series, and in the Marvel Universe, she was an opponent of both Dracula and Dr. Strange. Marie Laveau also appears in video games: she is investigated in the game *Gabriel Knight* and is mentioned in *BloodRayne*.

Marie Laveau is a character in numerous songs of various genres, some of which are even named after the Voodoo Queen herself. Want to listen to a few of the songs dedicated to Marie Laveau? Visit the link in the footnote to listen to the playlist we have prepared especially for you![90]

Leadership after Marie Laveau

As the late 1880s faded into the dawn of the new century, the columns of New Orleans newspapers listed a multitude of women who had captured public interest. Among these figures were Mama Caroline, Madame Frazie, and Malvina Latour, each seemingly poised to fill the void that had been left by Marie Laveau. Interestingly, there was no evidence that indicated any of Marie's daughters had stepped forward as the new Voodoo Queen.[91]

---

90. https://open.spotify.com/playlist/5zQLRowKqRVbF2NnaOPGZ S?si=fb59d6c6156c4503

91. Long, "Marie Laveau Timeline."

Although Marie Laveau's daughter, Marie Philomène, became the main figure of Voodoo after Marie Laveau's death, it was Malvina Latour who held the title of Queen of Voodoo in New Orleans. One newspaper stated, "Marie Laveau is dead; Malvina Latour is queen."[92]

Marie Laveau Today

The late twentieth century saw a greater acceptance of Voodoo as a religion and of Marie Laveau, who evolved from a terrifying witch character to the beloved mother goddess of New Orleans. But despite this belated interest in Marie as an important figure, scholars considered the topic to be of little relevance, and decided it did not merit the arduous research needed to uncover the factual data. This changed in the 1990s and 2000s, when scholars began to move beyond stereotypes and reexamine the role of Marie Laveau. We would like to highlight some of the scholars who dedicated themselves to this research:

Asbury, Herbert. *The French Quarter: An Informal History of the New Orleans Underworld.*

Daggett, Melissa. *Spiritualism in Nineteenth-Century New Orleans: The Life and Times of Henry Louis Rey.*

Dillon, Catherine. Unpublished "Voodoo" Manuscript.

---

92. For more of this article, see https://www.newspapers.com/article /st-joseph-saturday-herald-st-joseph-he/22140585.

Duggal, Barbara Rosendale. "Marie Laveau: The Voodoo Queen Repossessed."

Fandrich, Ina Johanna. *The Mysterious Voodoo Queen, Marie Laveaux: A Study of Powerful Female Leadership in Nineteenth-Century New Orleans.*

Sussman, Rachelle. "Conjuring Marie Laveau: The Syncretic Life of a Nineteenth-Century Voodoo Priestess in America."

Ward, Martha. *Voodoo Queen: The Spirited Lives of Marie Laveau.*

Although the mention of her name still gives some the chills, Marie Laveau, due to her magical deeds and kindness, came to be worshipped as a Lwa of New Orleans Voodoo and Hoodoo.

Marie Laveau's Veve

She is a benevolent and tremendously powerful spirit, helping everyone with love and affection, particularly in matters of love and in the purification or spiritual cleansing of people and places. To ask for Marie's blessings, you can make a simple offering, consisting of a light pink or light blue candle, a glass with sweet liqueur (anisette is the most used), sweets (chocolates, candies, milk pudding), cigarillos, and delicate and fragrant flowers. If possible, draw Marie Laveau's veve with chalk or white *pemba* on the floor or a wooden board. If you prefer, you can draw it with a pencil on a piece of paper, as Hoodoo practitioners usually use any material they have on hand.

Marie Laveau's International Shrine

The International Shrine of Marie Laveau is a spiritual and artistic project within the New Orleans Healing Center. It is centered around a statue of Marie Laveau created by Ricardo Pustanio and presented to the International Shrine of Marie Laveau so that fans and visitors have an appropriate place to leave offerings and perform prayers. The shrine is located at the following address: 2372 St. Claude Avenue, New Orleans, LA 70117.

CHAPTER 6
OTHER IMPORTANT CHARACTERS IN NEW ORLEANS VOODOO

This chapter covers three more names that are infamous in New Orleans: Malvina Latour, Lala, and Dr. John.

Malvina Latour

Malvina Frappier Latour was born in 1878. She was the daughter of Moise Bailard Latour and Marcelline Blais. She was described as a beautiful woman with a large physique. It is reported that she had darker skin than Marie Laveau I and Marie Laveau II. She was sometimes confused with them and called "Marie Laveau," making her, in a sense, a sort of Marie Laveau III.

Malvina was a striking character. She liked to wear blue dresses with white dots and a beautiful scarlet and orange tignon. One of her first actions as Voodoo Queen was unsuccessful: she intended to exclude Catholic rites from Voodoo, but to this day, Voodoo and Catholicism coexist peacefully. Malvina was Catholic and stated that she practiced Voodoo as a way of life, not as a religion.[93] She replaced Marie Laveau II in many ceremonies and soon created a clientele of her own.

Reports indicate that in 1870, in a crowded Black church, Malvina performed a spectacular feat: she miraculously cured Reverend Turner, who was suffering from an incurable illness. People came to her home in search of healing, financial prosperity, and love. She did not reach the popularity of Marie Laveau and Marie Laveau II, though she generally reproduced the practices of both, nor did she produce gris-gris as efficient as those of the Laveaus.

After the death of Marie Laveau and Marie Laveau II, New Orleans Voodoo fragmented into several parts with many leaders. Malvina was unable to keep the practice intact and, by the late nineteenth century, she did not lead the majority of Voodoo practices in New Orleans. However, she continued to be very important in the New Orleans Voodoo scene.

Malvina Latour died in 1959 and was buried at Precious Blood Cemetery in Rhode Island.

Lala, the Queen's Heir

During the nineteenth century, Voodoo Queens became prominent figures in New Orleans, commanding ceremo-

---

93. Interestingly, this is true of many practitioners. Catholicism is their religion, and Vodou/Voodoo is their spiritual practice.

nies and rituals. They survived by preparing charms, amulets, and magical powders to cure illnesses and meet the most varied requests.

In the late 1970s, Irma Thomas, a singer from New Orleans, recorded a song called "Princess La La" based on Lala, whose real name was Laura Hunter. (This song can be heard in the playlist linked in chapter 5.) In this song, Irma Thomas sings details about the famous Voodoo Queen who reigned in New Orleans in the 1930s and 1940s. Some writers believed that if a living successor to the Voodoo throne of Marie Laveau was to be identified, it would likely be Lala.[94]

It was acknowledged by Lala herself that she faced a multitude of challenges. She found herself subjected to various attempts to exert influence over her, yet none of those efforts proved effective. On one occasion, Lala told a judge that if he gave her his ring, she could make it walk. As Lala walked away holding the ring, the judge expressed his admiration for her astuteness.[95]

Dr. John Montanee

John Montanee was better known as Dr. John or Jean Bayou and was one of the people who introduced Voodoo to New Orleans. He pioneered the sale of potions

---

94. Tallant, *Voodoo in New Orleans*.

95. Tallant, *Voodoo in New Orleans*.

and gris-gris in New Orleans. He is revered as a Lwa by some; he is the protector of Voodoo men and rootwomen (women who practice Hoodoo).

Little was written about his life until the publication of the book *Dr. John Montanee: A Grimoire* by Louie Martinié, a work that richly documents the evolution of New Orleans Voodoo in the twenty-first century. In one essay in *Dr. John Montanee*, Denise Alvarado carefully examined Dr. John's signature for clues as to the type of person he was. She believed his signature indicated a resolute and industrious soul who wanted to achieve greatness and skillfully navigated life's challenges.[96] Dr. John's personal odyssey involved harrowing experiences of abduction, enslavement, and involuntary relocation to an alien terrain (Cuba), which serve as testaments to his unwavering fortitude and remarkable capacity for adjustment.

When Dr. John was an enslaved man in Cuba, his inner fortitude led to his freedom. After much training, Dr. John ascended to a level of culinary expertise that garnered respect and paved the way for his emancipation. Then, he embarked on a transformative journey. He left Cuba and embarked on a maritime voyage, where he assumed the role of the ship's cook. His voyage led him to New Orleans, and it was here that his attributes of physical fortitude, charisma, and unyielding resolve pro-

---

96. Alvarado, "The Superposition of Dr. Jean."

pelled him to a position of leadership amongst a group of laborers. Within this close-knit community, he became known for his extraordinary supernatural abilities and remarkable foresight, which laid the foundation for his outstanding accomplishments in the city of New Orleans.

Over time, Dr. John became a legend in New Orleans, a respected gris-gris man with many possessions. Legend has it that he had many loves and was a great healer, combining Catholic practices with Voodoo.

An 1862 edition of New Orleans newspaper *The Times-Picayune* provides a glimpse into Dr. John's personal life:

> PROVOST COURT—John Montanet, a free man of color, was yesterday before the Court as an applicant for his daughter's freedom. From the pleadings before the Court it would appear that Montanet lived with a slave woman, by whom he had two children, one of whom died, and the other—the subject of the application—is now about eleven years of age. It was in proof that Montanet intended to procure the freedom of his wife and had paid $600 to her owner, but that the act of manumission had never been perfected. The daughter, too, had been taken to Cincinnati, where she was baptized by a priest. According to

the laws of Louisiana, the status of a child is governed by the condition of the mother, and the girl was consequently a slave. Being in financial difficulties, Montanet executed a mortgage on his slave daughter, and under this mortgage she was sold in February to Mr. Salvoie. It was to set aside this sale and establish the freedom of his daughter that this suit was brought, and though Mr. Roselins, for the defence, claimed that the sale was legal and should not be overturned, the Judge thought otherwise and decreed that the girl was free.[97]

Working with Dr. John

To begin with, it is best not to ask Dr. John for any favors. Just give him some offerings and start developing a relationship with him. When he makes his presence known to you through dreams, visions, and physical manifestations, then it will be the appropriate time to begin making requests of him.

Offerings to Dr. John

• Absinthe liqueur

• Graveyard dirt

---

97. This newspaper clipping was found at https://www.newspapers.com /article/the-times-picayune-john-montanee-applies/21720229.

- High John Root (*Ipomoea purga*, or the Jalapa root)
- Low John Root (*Trillium pendulum*, or Bethroot)
- Red brick powder
- Herbs and healing roots in general
- Gris-gris

For those who want to learn more about Voodoo and Hoodoo, we recommend Denise Alvarado's work *The Voodoo Hoodoo Spellbook*.

CHAPTER 7
HOODOO

Hoodoo is a traditional form of African American folk magic. Generally, its adherents are called *conjurers* and *rootworkers*. In general, Hoodoo could be said to be a union of three traditional aspects of magic, healing, and folklore of European immigrants: Haitian Vodou; the knowledge about herbs and healing of the North American Natives; and the set of magical techniques and wisdom compiled from some European grimoires such as the *Grimorium Verum*, *The Grimoire of Pope Honorius*, *The Book of Abramelin*, and even *The Keys of Solomon*. Hoodoo was also heavily influenced by L. W. de Laurence's book *The Great Book of Magical Arts, Hindu Magic, and East Indian Occultism*[98] and *The Long-Lost Friend*, a famous American grimoire of the nineteenth century.

---

98. This book is published nowadays as *The Obeah Bible*.

The word *Hoodoo* was first recorded in the English language in 1868, used to describe a spell or magic potion.[99] Hoodoo was born in the oppressive environment experienced by enslaved Americans, and some of them brought ancestral knowledge from their tribes; others learned from enslaved people who fled the Caribbean, roughly called *marons*. Lacking the liturgical elements they were accustomed to in their traditions, they began to make use of any item that was within reach. An example of this was the replacement of statues carved in iroko wood with ordinary dolls of cloth or wax. Due to its very humble origins, Hoodoo stands out among other magical traditions precisely because it works with common elements that anyone has in their home (or at least *had*, when these practices became known). Usually, the conjurer works in his own house, although there are two other places that are essential to the practice of Hoodoo: the crossroads and the cemetery.

Anyone who intends to study and practice Hoodoo in Brazil encounters some difficulty, either because several traditional plants are found only in the flora of North America, or because it is very common to use ready-made recipes for powders and baths, sold in stores, called botanicals. Still, with some effort, it is possible to acquire these

---

99. *Merriam-Webster*, s.v. "hoodoo (*n.*)," accessed December 12, 2023, https://www.merriam-webster.com/dictionary/hoodoo.

herbs and learn the recipes for some baths and powders, such as the ones we will present later in this chapter.

Unlike formal religions, Hoodoo does not have a structured hierarchy. It also does not present a theology, established priests and laypeople, or proper liturgical work orders. Its adherents are almost always secular people within a Christian community who have some type of specific knowledge of magic and the Hoodoo tradition. Its practices can be adapted to various forms of religious worship. In short, Hoodoo is not religion—it is a way of life. A traditional Hoodoo healer used to be a nomadic individual who traveled from town to town selling their work, sometimes setting up a store in the communities.

Basically, three religious influences on Hoodoo can be identified: Catholicism, Protestantism, and Voodoo. Still, even though Hoodoo has excluded any and all religions from its practices, its adherent must have a religion, faith, or belief in something greater: God, Goddess, Lwa, Orisha, etc. In New Orleans, Hoodoo is strongly influenced by Catholicism, with recipes that use the power of the saints being very common (among the most famous, Saint Expeditus, Saint Anthony, and Saint Cyprian). In Protestant states, recipes use a lot of recitation of verses from the Bible and the Psalms, whereas where there is the influence of Voodoo, as occurs throughout Louisiana, it is common to appeal to Lwas such as Erzulie, Papa Legba, Ogou, and Maman Brigitte.

Another characteristic of Hoodoo is that there is no need for any initiation ceremony. The conjurer or root-worker practices what they learned from their family or their masters without having undergone any formal initiation or even sacramental blessing.

Hoodoo is often confused with Voodoo, as they have a lot in common, but they are different things. Voodoo is a religion, and Hoodoo is an African American practice of folk magic that can also be a complement to faith. A practitioner often views Hoodoo as a kind of personal power that can help themselves or others through knowledge of herbs, minerals, animal parts, bodily fluids, and possessions.

Hoodoo uses many Voodoo techniques regarding the use of magic (oils, powders, dolls, etc.). In addition to the famous cloth or wax dolls used for all purposes, mojo bags (also known as gris-gris) are very typical of Hoodoo, which are bags containing herbs, stones, bones, or animal skin to attract something to its holder; the curios, which are items of animal origin, such as crocodile teeth, rabbit's foot, snakeskin, and black cat hair; as well as oils with very curious names, as depicted on the website of the famous botanist catherine yronwode,[100] also known as dressing

---

100. See http://www.luckymojo.com/oils.html.

oils or greasing oils. It is said that Psychic Vision Oil brings prophetic dreams and visions, Constant Work Oil helps the user remain employed, and John the Conqueror Root Oil (*Ipomoea purga*, or the Jalapa root) is known to be able to increase and strengthen sexual potency.

Van-Van Oil is the most famous of all the other formulas from New Orleans and Algiers, Louisiana. It is used to undo spells cast by enemies, dispel evil, bring good luck, and increase the power of amulets and talismans. Its preparation method is as follows: Mix a pinch of lemongrass and a pinch of salt into a glass containing olive oil; the glass should be placed in water until lukewarm. After that, the oil should be stored in a dark place for at least thirty days. Both the ingredients and the oil must be consecrated, and for this purpose, the same method taught for the making of gris-gris can be used, which will be explained later in the chapter.

Brief Hoodoo, Conjure, and Rootwork Recipes

1 | Vinegar is excellent for fighting negative energies, the evil eye, and bad luck. For these purposes, you can wash the doors of your home with the following mixture: In a bucket containing water, add half a glass of wine vinegar, four tablespoons of table

salt, and a squeezed lemon. Pray Psalm 23 [101] after mixing the ingredients. Apply the mixture to the doors of your home using a cloth. After the doors have dried naturally, you can also cross them, making a small cross on each door with olive oil also prepared with the recitation of Psalm 23.

2 | To get rid of an enemy, take a white candle and pass it all over your body, starting at the head and ending at the feet. As you do so, pray for deliverance from the enemy. Once done, light the candle and recite aloud Nehemiah 9:27-28. Let the candle burn out completely.

3 | If you need to ask for justice against someone who has harmed you in some way, light a red candle, recite 2 Samuel 22:49-50, and say your request aloud.

4 | If you are wanting to recover a lost love, cover a small table or altar with a bright red fabric and arrange lilies, red wine, a red seven-day candle, and a photo of the loved one. Arrange the lilies, wine, and candle in a triangular shape (the candle at the top, the wine on the right, and the lilies on the left). Draw a heart on the photo using red

---

101. For this and all other biblical verses in this section, we recommend you refer to the King James Version of the Bible.

paint or pen, and place it in the center of the triangle. Pray to Saint Anthony, asking him to bring your love back. Repeat the prayer every day until the candle is finished burning.

5 | To vanquish a lawsuit unfairly brought against you, set aside an orange seven-day candle, a new rosary, a bowl, dust taken from the forum or court, and dust or dirt taken from the traffic light closest to your home. On a table, place the bowl containing both powders, placing the rosary around it. Knock the candle's base on the table three times and ask Saint Peter to protect you from the unfair accusation and make you win the case. Also, ask him to bless the rosary, transferring his power of protection to it. Light the candle inside the bowl. You must repeat the prayer three times a day until the candle has finished burning. After that, take the rosary and tie it to your car's rearview mirror[102] or carry it with you.

6 | If you need to attract money, get a cloth napkin, a white candle, powdered bay leaf, ground cinnamon, sugar, olive oil over which Psalm 23 was recited, and a paper on which you will write your

---

102. In some states, it is illegal to hang objects from your rearview mirror. Research your state's laws before hanging anything from your mirror.

request for money. Spread the napkin on a table. Burn the paper you wrote on and mix its ashes with the powdered bay leaf, ground cinnamon, and sugar. Write your name on the candle from bottom to top (you can use the tip of a knife, a pin, or a needle), anoint it with consecrated olive oil or Van-Van Oil (in Hoodoo, this is called "dressing" the candle), and roll the candle over the powdered mixture. Then, hold the candle close to your mouth and say a prayer to God asking for money. Light the candle, and after it burns out, bury any remaining wax in your yard or a park.

7 | Coffee is immensely powerful when you want to do a spiritual cleansing and remove any blockages that are in your path. A traditional way to use its properties is to prepare the following bath: a glass of strong coffee, four tablespoons of salt, and the juice of a lemon. After mixing these items in a bucket or container, add them to bathwater and recite Isaiah 54:17. Then, take your bath and let the mixture dry on you naturally for about ten minutes. After that, take a shower or bathe as usual.

8 | It is very common to use mojo bags or gris-gris, which are nothing more than bags containing

plant, mineral, and animal items that serve to attract what their owner needs.

Here is a mojo bag recipe to attract money and prosperity: Take a piece of green flannel or raw cotton fabric, a little cotton string, two pinches of crushed dried thyme, a pinch of cinnamon, a small magnet, a little piece of orange peel, a piece of jalapa root, three grains of black-eyed peas, and a dollar bill. You will also need a plate, a candle, a glass of water, a glass of rum or whiskey, a cigar, and Allspice Oil—that is, oil with allspice. (This oil should be prepared a month in advance: Fill a glass halfway with allspice, then finish filling it with olive oil. Warm it in water without letting it boil, then store the glass in a dark place for a month.)

To make the bag, light a candle to illuminate your work, place a glass of water next to it, and mix the herbs in a container. Waft cigar smoke over the herbs and sprinkle them with rum or whiskey. Present the container with the herbs to the four cardinal points and say your prayers. A powerful prayer for this work is the recitation of Deuteronomy 28:13. Place the herbs on the cloth and talk to them. (For example, "Cinnamon, be the fire in this work that will bring me prosperity.

Jalapa, bring money to me.") Offer the herbs again to the four cardinal points. Close the bag with the string, making seven turns, while continuing to make your requests. When you are finished, tie three knots in the string. You can carry this bag in your pocket, or if you want to make it even more powerful, go to a bench where there is a garden or area of land, dig a small hole in the ground, put three coins in as payment for the spiritual work, and bury the bag. Three days later, dig up the bag and carry it with you.

9 | To make a protective powder, you will need talcum powder (or rice powder), rue, angelica, rosemary, white sage, and bay leaf. (All herbs should be dry.) Grind the herbs until they become a fine powder and mix with the talcum powder. Do not forget to pray for protection and talk to the herbs to determine their purpose. When done, recite Psalm 23 over the powder.

10 | Another recipe is focused on prosperity in the home. Take some dust from the doorstep of your home, some dirt from the crossroads closest to your house, sugar, ground cinnamon, and pieces of a ripped-up dollar bill.[103] Mix everything together,

---

103. In the US, defacing currency is considered unlawful. Use your discretion.

and starting at the front door of your home, sprinkle the mixture toward the back door of your home. (Do not sprinkle the mixture onto carpet.) Let it rest for a few minutes and then, using a broom, sweep everything from the back door to the front. Sweep up the entire mixture and throw it in the center of the same crossroads.

11 | In many houses in the southern United States, you may see chicken feet hanging on the door as a protective amulet. In fact, chicken feet are an essential element of Hoodoo practices. You can get them from a poultry farm and dry them carefully in the sun. Once dry, you can use your chicken feet to spiritually cleanse yourself or others. To do so, simply pass the chicken foot all over the body and then turn it counterclockwise in your hands. (If you are doing the cleansing on yourself, you should also turn counterclockwise.) While doing this, repeat the first verse of Psalm 23.

12 | Suppose you do not want unwanted visitors to return to your home. Spread a mixture of ground black pepper and salt on the floor near your front door. After a few moments, sweep the dust out of your home.

13 | Owners of houses open to the public and businesses in general can protect them from envy,

bad luck, and any evil by sprinkling the powder of crushed, dried Boldo leaves on-site once a month.

14 | If you want to cleanse a place without smoking it, place a small piece of camphor in each corner and let it evaporate naturally.

15 | To have good luck in a game or competition, on a test, or in any endeavor, wash your hands with chamomile tea while reciting Psalm 23.

16 | To cleanse a house where there have been incidents of violence, murder, suicide, or a strong infestation of lower astral forces, incense it for fourteen days with a mixture of cinnamon, sandalwood, myrrh, and frankincense.

One of the most traditional Hoodoo recipes is "Four Thieves Vinegar," used for spiritual cleansing and protection from harmful magic. Next, we will share two recipes for it. The first, simpler version consists of crushing a handful of peeled garlic, putting it in a glass, and filling the glass with red wine vinegar.

The other, more laborious version involves crushing the same handful of garlic with some cloves, rue leaves, and sage leaves and placing the resulting mass in a jar. Pour a glass of brandy and dissolve a tablet of camphor in it, then add this to the jar. Finally, fill the rest of the jar with red wine vinegar.

Regardless of which recipe you use, the mixture should rest in a dark place for a month before use.

17 | To keep people away from a place, mix white carnation petals with Four Thieves Vinegar and spray the mixture while reciting Psalm 37:1.

18 | An effective way to stop gossip and slander is to stick several cloves into a red candle and light it with this intent.

19 | If you want to get rid of addictions such as smoking or drinking alcohol, regularly take baths with eucalyptus leaves.

20 | To ensure marital happiness, make a mixture of lavender flowers and rose petals or buds and place it under the couple's bed.

21 | If a man is mistreating a woman and she wants to get rid of him, she should buy a new knife and get a fresh lemon. Then, without being noticed, she should follow him, cutting pieces of the lemon and throwing them in his wake. Once this is done, she should return home, bury the knife near her doorstep, and say: "In the name of the Father, the Son, and the Holy Spirit, I never want to see [Name] again." If the man in question realizes what the

woman is doing, she must repeat the entire process again, including acquiring another knife.

22 | Lucky rice is a widespread resource in the Southern United States. The method is simple: Put grains of rice in your everyday shoes and do not remove the rice for seventy-two hours straight. (Naturally, you should wear only these shoes during the seventy-two-hour period.) After that, spread the grains on the floor of your house, then sweep them up. Spread this rice around your business or on your land.

23 | To be happy in a new home, discard the salt and broom you used in the old house halfway through the move. Enter the new house with a new broom and a new bag of salt.

24 | Violet leaves are used to attract new love. To do this, put a violet leaf in your everyday shoes and do not remove the leaves until seven days have passed. (Of course, you should wear only these shoes during the seven-day period.) Then, carry these leaves in your wallet or purse.

Make Gris-Gris Yourself

Gris-gris is a very traditional talisman in Louisiana Hoodoo and Voodoo. It is a small bag of fabric, usually red in color, in which various objects are placed to attract what its owner wants. There are gris-gris, therefore, for health, protection, luck, money, and love.

Some argue that the origin of the word is African— specifically, Ghanaian—and derives from the habit of Black Muslims carrying talismans in bags containing excerpts from the Qur'an. Others maintain that the word *gris-gris* came from the way enslaved Americans spoke the French word *grise*, "gray," since they used to make their talismans with the gray fabric they were given to sew clothes.

Here, we will teach you how to make a gris-gris for protection and good luck. You will need the following items:

- A piece of flannel or red felt
- Angelica
- Hyssop
- Lemongrass
- Jalapa
- A little coarse salt

Angelica, hyssop, and lemongrass are plants tradition-ally associated with protection, balance, and purification. Coarse salt is a mineral element whose function is to repel evil. Jalapa, known as High John the Conqueror, is the most relevant plant in Hoodoo and is used to attract luck and power.

Firstly, you should sew your gris-gris bag as follows:

1 | Take a piece of flannel or red felt and cut it into the shape of a rectangle.

2 | Cut a piece a little smaller than the last so that when they are laid on top of each other, there is a small border. This becomes your seam allowance.

3 | Sew the rectangles on top of each other, leaving one side open.

4 | Make four small cuts, one in each corner of the bag, without damaging the sewing, then turn the bag inside out.[104]

Once this is done, place all the items on a clean surface and sprinkle them with holy water. Here, you can choose between using holy water obtained from a church or blessing the water yourself using the Hoodoo method. In the case of the latter, simply mix a little salt in a container of water and, laying your hands on the container, recite Psalm 23.

---

104. If you are more of a visual learner, search YouTube for pillow sewing tutorials. One such video with helpful visuals can be found at https://www.youtube.com/watch?v=GhUrDlSHNZg.

Light a white candle, which will represent the divine light that is always shining on your life and your paths. If you have Van-Van Oil, a traditional Hoodoo oil, you can anoint your candle with it, but this is not essential.

Take the ingredients into your hands one by one and present them to the four quadrants—north, south, east, and west—saying aloud the purpose for which you are using that ingredient. Remember that powerful ancestral spirits and beings linked to the forces of nature will hear your call and come to your aid if you are imbued with pure purposes.

Fill your bag with the ingredients and, as you finish sewing it closed, stitch three stitches inward and three stitches outward—that is, three stitches in the direction of your body and three stitches in the opposite direction. The former will attract the good fortune you are asking for, while the latter will repel evil and opposing forces.

Leave your gris-gris next to the candle, and when it burns out, start carrying the bag with you every day, preferably next to your body.

The Use of Psalms in Hoodoo

The tradition of using the Psalms for magical purposes is strong in the United States, the result of the folklore brought by the Germans who settled in the region of Pennsylvania and whose set of ancient knowledge was called Powwow. The absorption of the magical use of the Psalms by Hoodoo took place through practitioners whose religious background was Protestantism. In the beginning of the twentieth century, the book *Secrets of the Psalms: A Fragment of the Practical Kabala* by Godfrey A. Selig was published in English and was very successful among practitioners of popular magic. Other books that greatly contributed to the spread of this practice were the eighteenth-century grimoire known as *The Sixth and Seventh Books of Moses* as well as the aforementioned books by John George Hohman.

Next, the magical purposes of each psalm will be indicated, as well as the recommended color of candle to use; when more than one candle color is indicated in the same psalm, it should be noted that they follow the sequence of objectives indicated for each of them. In any case, a white candle or an oil lamp can be used for any occasion.

PSALM	CANDLE	PURPOSE
1	Red	Risky pregnancy
2	Pink	Danger at sea or in stormy weather
3	Blue	Headaches
4	Green	Good luck

PSALM	CANDLE	PURPOSE
5	Violet	Relations with the government and bureaucracies
6	Blue	Eye diseases
7	Violet	Undo a spell
8	Green	Success in business and commercial transactions
9	Blue; Violet	Sick child; protection from evil and enemies
10	Violet	Keep away evil souls and evil spirits
11	Violet	Protection against oppression and persecution
12	Violet	Protection against oppression and persecution
13	Violet	Stay safe for twenty-four hours
14	Pink; Violet	Gain trust and favor; protection from corrupt people
15	Violet	Depression
16	Red	Happiness
17	Violet	Travel protection

PSALM	CANDLE	PURPOSE
18	Violet	Protection against thieves
19	Blue	Serious illness
20	Violet	To avoid danger and suffering for a day
21	Violet	Storm at sea
22	Violet	Storms and earthly dangers
23	White; Blue	Blessings; divination and dreams
24	Red	Gain strength against the opposition
25	Red	Gain strength against the opposition
26	Green	Unemployment
27	Pink	Be well-received in a new place
28	Pink	Make peace with someone you do not get along with
29	Violet	Gain power
30	Violet	Get rid of evil
31	Violet	Against slander

PSALM	CANDLE	PURPOSE
32	Violet	Divine forgiveness, grace, and love
33	Red	Avoid the death of a young child
34	Green	Obtain favors from important people
35	Violet	Judicial issues
36	Violet	Judicial issues
37	Blue	Alcoholism
38	Violet	Against slander
39	Violet	Against slander
40	Red	Make wishes come true
41	Violet	Regain trust after being slandered
42	Blue	Receive instructions in dreams
43	Violet	Regain trust after being slandered
44	Violet	Protection from enemies
45	Red; Pink	Bring love and passion; reestablish love and marital peace

PSALM	CANDLE	PURPOSE
46	Red; Pink	Bring love and passion; reestablish love and marital peace
47	Pink	Be loved
48	Violet	Protection against envy
49	Blue	Fever
50	Blue	Fever
51	White	Cleansing and purification
52	Violet	Get rid of slander
53	Violet	Get rid of enemy pursuits
54	Violet	Get rid of enemy pursuits
55	Violet	Get rid of enemy pursuits
56	Violet	Material problems
57	Green	Attract money
58	Pink	Communing in peace with animals and nature
59	Violet	Spiritual possession
60	Violet	Protection during war
61	Green	Bless a new home
62	Violet	Forgive someone

PSALM	CANDLE	PURPOSE
63	Violet	Get rid of a contract
64	Green	Sea trip
65	Green	Blessings and luck in ventures
66	Violet	Obsessions and compulsions
67	Violet	Protection against bad events
68	Violet	Protection against bad events
69	Violet	Break bad habits
70	Violet	Break bad habits
71	Violet	Free someone from slavery
72	Green	Prosperity and good relationships
73	Green	All-purpose
74	Green	All-purpose
75	Green	All-purpose
76	Green	All-purpose
77	Green	All-purpose
78	Green	All-purpose
79	Green	All-purpose
80	Green	All-purpose

PSALM	CANDLE	PURPOSE
81	Green	All-purpose
82	Green	All-purpose
83	Green	All-purpose
84	Blue	Chronic diseases
85	Pink	Restore peace between two friends
86	Green	Help someone succeed
87	Green	Help someone succeed
88	Green	Help someone succeed
89	Blue	Healing from a distance
90	Violet	Tame wild animals and protect the house
91	Violet	Protection against evil
92	Green	Earn respect
93	Violet	Judicial issues
94	Violet	Gain power over an enemy
95	Violet	Prevent a friend from making a serious mistake

PSALM	CANDLE	PURPOSE
96	Green	Happiness and blessings for the family
97	Green	Happiness and blessings for the family
98	Pink	Peace in the family
99	Blue	Develop inner power
100	Violet	Protection from unknown enemies
101	Violet	The evil eye
102	Red	Fertility
103	Red	Fertility
104	Violet	Melancholy
105	Blue	Fever
106	Blue	Fever
107	Blue	Fever
108	Green	Abundance in the home
109	Violet	Defeat a powerful enemy
110	Violet	Gain charm and charisma
111	Violet	Gain charm and charisma

PSALM	CANDLE	PURPOSE
112	Violet	Balance and harmony
113	Violet	Balance and harmony
114	Green	Success in business
115	Violet	Better teaching
116	Violet	General safety
117	Violet	Prevent thoughtless words
118	Violet	Increase willpower
119	Violet; Violet; Blue; Blue	Increase intelligence and improve memory (verses 9 to 16); help in spiritual life (verses 33 to 41); help a friend overcome melancholy (verses 49 to 56); hip pain, kidney or liver problems (verses 65 to 72)
120	Violet	Fair judgment
121	Violet	Safety during an evening trip
122	Violet	Gain the favor of authority
123	Pink; Yellow	Keep friends close; look good at a formal event
124	Violet	Safety when traveling by water

PSALM	CANDLE	PURPOSE
125	Violet	Gain power over enemies
126	Violet	Bless and protect children
127	Violet	Bless and protect children
128	Violet	Protect a pregnancy
129	Violet	Gain spiritual power
130	Violet	Escape from danger
131	Violet	Overcome pride
132	Violet	Prevent thoughtless words
133	Pink	Win and earn true friends
134	Violet	The success of a party and exemplary performance on tests and exams
135	White	Protection against temptations
136	Violet	Break cycles of negativity
137	Violet	Overcome resentment
138	Pink	Attract love
139	Red	Intensify a couple's love
140	Violet	Marriage issues
141	Violet	Overcome fear

PSALM	CANDLE	PURPOSE
142	Blue	Pain in the arms and legs
143	Blue	Pain in the arms and legs
144	Blue	Fractures
145	Violet	Ward off evil spirits
146	Blue	Wounds
147	Blue	Infections
148	Violet	Protection from fire
149	Violet	Protection from fire
150	Red	Turn sadness into joy

Traditional Hoodoo Prayer to Open Paths

A prayer is often said while lighting the popular seven-day candles sold by metaphysical stores in the United States. A traditional Hoodoo prayer opens paths to money, health, success, love, and happiness. The exact phrases vary depending on who wrote the prayer, so if a candle comes with a pre-written incantation, you may use that instead. Here is one example of an Open Path prayer:

> Divine Creator, I come to you with an open heart and an open mind. I ask for your guidance and support as I embark on this new journey.

I pray that you help me to clear away any obstacles that may be in my path, and to create a clear and open road before me. Please help me to trust in your divine plan and to have faith in the journey ahead.

May your light shine upon me and guide me towards the path that is in alignment with my highest good. May your love and grace surround me and lift me up, giving me the strength and courage I need to face any challenges that may come my way.

With gratitude in my heart, I thank you for the blessings you have bestowed upon me and for the blessings yet to come. I trust in your infinite wisdom and love, and I am ready to walk this path with your divine guidance.

Amen.[105]

Hoodoo's Most Traditional Recipes

It would be impossible to cover all the traditional recipes of Hoodoo, both because this book serves as just an introduction to the topic and because one cannot hope to exhaust an entire popular tradition, especially one as old

---

105. This prayer accompanies the Open Road 7 Day Candle sold by Original Botanica (https://originalbotanica.com/open-road-7 -day-prayer-candle).

as Hoodoo. Proof of this is that not even the monumental work of Harry Middleton Hyatt managed to cover the entire vast field of the Hoodoo tradition.

Hyatt was an Anglican pastor who, in his spare time, had the folklore of the Southern United States as a hobby. He dedicated himself to compiling hundreds of interviews with practitioners throughout the 1950s into five thick volumes. This work, entitled *Hoodoo, Conjuration, Witchcraft, Rootwork*, is the most complete collection of recipes, spells, prayers, and traditional practices, therefore proving to be unbelievably valuable for anyone who wants to truly delve into this rich and multicolored universe of North American folk magic.

Among the plethora of Hoodoo recipes, the most well-known categories are those involving floor washing and baths, pots of honey (and sugar), spells in jars and bottles in general, spells placed inside shoes, and bewitched foods. Thus, in addition to the Hoodoo recipes included in this book, we will give some very practical (and infallible) examples of these traditional variants.

Let's go!

The Waters of Hoodoo

In the universe of Hoodoo tradition, nothing is vaster than the set of recipes involving magical waters (or *conjure waters*). There are very simple recipes for floor washing;

for example, mixing indigo with water, or holy water, or Florida Water[106] or even lavender tea (*Lavandula angustifolia*), or hyssop (*Hyssopus officinalis*). Whether you use these waters to effectively wash the floor, pour buckets of water onto the ground, or use them to wet the cloth that will be passed over the floor of your home or business, the fact is that a Hoodoo practitioner never uses ordinary water for cleaning, but will always add one or more of the ingredients listed above to ensure spiritual cleansing and the protection of the place, as well as to attract good luck and happiness.

There are a few more elaborate recipes, like this bath for opening paths and clearing energy blockages.

Ingredients

2 white candles

A handful of hyssop (*Hyssopus officinalis*)

A handful of rue (*Ruta graveolens*)

A handful of agrimony (*Agrimonia eupatoria*)

A plate

1 cigar

---

106. Florida Water is a nineteenth-century multipurpose cologne in Hoodoo. There are two versions: the American, more citrusy, and the Latin, sweeter and "hot," given the large amount of cinnamon used in the formula. It's not difficult to find Florida Water for sale on the internet or in a metaphysical shop.

1 glass of rum

Florida Water

A piece of white cloth to wrap your head

White bed linen

How To

Light one candle and pray Psalm 91. Place the herbs on a plate and present them to the four directions (east, west, north, and south), invoking your ancestral spirits.

Pray Psalm 51 and cleanse the herbs with cigar smoke, then wet them with rum. Macerate the herbs in cold water (if you have opted for fresh herbs) or make tea with them (if you have chosen dried herbs). Strain the mixture and add a little Florida Water. (Don't add too much!)

Add the mixture to the bathtub. Light the other white candle in the bathroom. Bathe from head to toe (yes, you should bathe your head too!), then wrap your head with the white cloth and lie down on the white bedding that you separated.

Stay lying down for at least one hour, if possible in prayer, making your requests to God and your ancestors.

Double Floor Wash

Another well-known recipe is a double floor wash to attract customers to your business and protect it from envy and the evil eye.

Ingredients

1 teaspoon of bergamot essential oil (*Citrus bergamia*)

1 teaspoon of clove essential oil (*Syzygium aromaticum*)

1 teaspoon of cedar essential oil (*Cedrela odorata*)

1 teaspoon of cinnamon essential oil (*Cinnamomum verum*)

1 teaspoon of sugar

Some of your fresh urine

How To

For the first floor wash, mix the essential oils of bergamot, clove, and cedar in a bucket of water and wash the floor of your commercial establishment from the inside out.

For the second wash, which must be done immediately after the first, mix the cinnamon essential oil, sugar, and a little of your urine, washing the floor from the outside to the inside. For obvious reasons, do not overdo the amount of urine! A few drops are enough.

❧ · ❧

There are also very curious recipes of widespread use, such as the following.

A Wash to Attract Customers to a Nightclub

Put some sugar on the left foot of a man's shoe and burn it until it is reduced to ashes. Mix these ashes with the water used to wash the floor, adding a tablespoon of sugar, a tablespoon of salt, and a tablespoon of your urine.

New Orleans Wash to Attract Customers to a Restaurant

In a large bucket containing water, mix a tablespoon of geranium essential oil (*Pelargonium graveolens*), a tablespoon of cinnamon essential oil (*Cinnamomum verum*), and a tablespoon of sugar. This water will be used to wash the sidewalk in front of the restaurant before its doors are opened to the public.

Hoodoo, Sweet Hoodoo!

Spells involving honey and sugar are legendary in Hoodoo, known as honey spells, sugar spells, and jar spells. Here we will share some very curious—and no less accurate—ones!

We will begin with two recipes shared by Zora Neale Hurston, a great American writer and anthropologist who was part of the Harlem Renaissance. Hurston was born at the end of the nineteenth century and died in 1960. She wrote classics such as *Their Eyes Were Watching God*; *Tell My Horse*; *Moses, Man of the Mountain*; and *Mules and Men*.

A Jar for Sweet Wishes

Fill a large jar with honey and sugar. Write your wishes on a piece of paper and place it inside the jar. You can insert as many wish papers as you want in this container. The best place to keep the jar is in the kitchen. Quite simple, right? Indeed, but it is extremely effective, so much so that this is one of the most popular Hoodoo recipes.

To Make People Love You

This recipe, as well as the Jar for Sweet Wishes, is based on one that appeared in Hurston's book *Mules and Men*.

Ingredients

9 teaspoons of corn starch

9 teaspoons of sugar

9 pinches of steel powder

Jockey Club Cologne [107] (or any other men's cologne)

9 wide pieces of white, blue, red, or yellow ribbon

Yellow thread

How To

Mix the powders and wet them with some of the cologne. Put a little bit of the mixture on a piece of ribbon and tie a knot, saying aloud the name of a person whose sympathy you want to win. Wrap the ribbon with the yellow thread, making knots while repeating the person's name.

---

107. This traditional cologne is used in betting and gambling. You can find it on the internet.

Repeat the process with the other eight pieces of ribbon, choosing a different person each time. Hide these nine bags made with ribbon in a closet, under a rug, or on a piece of furniture.

Let's now look at two recipes that involve jars of honey, the very traditional "honey jar spell."

A Honeypot for Love

Get a strand of your hair and a strand of hair from the one you love. On a piece of paper, write both of your names together and draw a heart on top. Roll the paper up and tie it with the two strands of hair.

Insert this rolled paper into a jar with honey, along with the petals of two red roses, saying: "Just as this honey is sweet on the tongue, so will I be sweet to [name of loved one]." Place the lid on the jar and light a red or pink candle on the lid.

Until your wish comes true, you can light a candle every Monday, Thursday, and Friday.

Honey Pot to Bring Peace to a Group of People

This spell can be used for any group of people: family, neighbors, colleagues, etc. Write people's names on a single piece of paper or write them on individual pieces of paper. Although it is not essential, try to get hair from these people. (This may seem difficult, but you will be surprised if you put masking tape or duct tape on the back of the chairs where they sit.)

Place the names (and strands of hair, if you have them) in a jar with honey, along with lavender (*Lavandula angustifolia*). Place the lid on the jar and light a white candle on the lid. You can light a new candle every Sunday and Thursday.

Stepping Hard!

Another Hoodoo "classic" is the varied set of spells involving pieces of paper placed inside a shoe. It can be said that this type of spell is an art in itself that must be properly studied, but here we will give some simple examples.

Paper in Shoe for a Job Interview

It is important to use a piece of paper that represents the company or place where you will be interviewed. You can obtain a business folder, if available, or print a page from the company's website. If you are right-handed, put your right foot on this sheet of paper and mark the outline of your foot with a pencil. If you are left-handed, do the same thing, but with your left foot.

Cut out the outline of your foot, but inside the shape drawn with the pencil so that the cutout fits inside your shoe. On this piece of paper, write verse nine of chapter eleven of the Gospel of Luke as follows: "So I say to you [your name]: Ask and it will be given to you [the name of the company or establishment]; seek and you will find [the position for which you want to be hired]; knock and the door will be opened to you [the position and the name of the company]."[108]

Draw dollar signs on this piece of paper. Dip your finger in olive oil and make a cross on the paper as well. Put this piece of paper in your right (if you are right-handed) or left (if you are left-handed) shoe and go confidently to your job interview!

To Win a Lawsuit

If you are involved in a legal process in which unfair accusations are being brought against you, do the following. Using a pen that can write on plastic surfaces (a permanent marker, for example), write the names of the twelve apostles on a sage leaf, bay leaf, or banana leaf: Simon Peter, Andrew, James (son of Zebedee), John, Philip, Bartholomew, Thomas, Matthew, James (son of Alpheus), Judas Thaddeus, Simon (the Zealot), and Judas Iscariot. Place the leaf inside your right shoe. Then, on a piece of paper, write the judge's name and place it inside your left shoe.

---

108. This phrasing and the other biblical quotes in this chapter are found in the King James Bible, but you may change the wording slightly depending on which version of the Bible you are using.

This spell is particularly useful on the day of a court hearing or a trial, but you can renew it whenever you want until you ensure your victory (or the case brought against you is dismissed).

For Protection

Write Psalm 91 on a piece of paper. Light a candle on the paper (placing it first on a small plate or in a candlestick) as you pray this psalm aloud nine times. Once the candle has burned out, place this piece of paper inside your left shoe whenever you need protection, especially when you have to go to a dangerous place.

To Dominate Someone

This spell is classic and obviously involves a good deal of ethical reflection. We recommend that it only be done in severe cases—where it is necessary to help someone overcome an addiction, for example. In any case, whatever your intention, take out a piece of paper. Write the person's name seven times, along with your intention and verse three of Psalm 47: "He shall subdue the people under us, and the nations under our feet."

Place this piece of paper inside your right shoe. Every time you remember the person, stomp your foot on the ground three times, saying the person's name aloud or in your head.

Bottle Spells

When it comes to magic bottles or "bottle spells," your creativity is the limit! You can create bottles for protection, prosperity, love, healing, or any goal you have in mind. With the two following examples, you can get an idea of how to work this way and even create your own spell. (Remember that Hoodoo recipes were not taught by God or His angels, but were created by everyday people.)

Bottle of Prosperity

Write your intention or desire on a piece of paper. Above it, write your name twice, in the shape of a cross. Place this rolled paper inside a bottle, in which you will also place gold dust, silver dust, a money note, cinnamon stick, bay leaves, cloves, a small pyrite, and a small magnet.

Once this is done, you will complete the bottle with a tea made with a money note, cinnamon stick, bay leaves, and cloves, to which you will add, after cooling, a dose of rum. Cap the bottle and light a candle over the bottle neck or next to it. Every day, shake the bottle, saying your wish out loud.

Bottle to Boost Your Psychic Powers

This bottle will help increase your psychic powers, whether you want to have lucid or prophetic dreams, make your oracle readings more accurate, awaken clairvoyance and telepathy, etc. To do so, decorate a bottle by pasting your photograph in place of the label. Paint astrological symbols (your moon sign is mandatory!), suits of cards, and any symbol that represents the psychic universe to you.

Inside the bottle place star anise, sage, mugwort, an amethyst, and a moonstone. Cover with water and add nine drops of jasmine or lavender essential oil. Leave the bottle outdoors for an entire night under the full moon so that it receives the moon's rays. After that, light a white or violet candle on Fridays, with the intention of increasing your psychic powers.

Now, let's get to the practical use of this bottle: if you want to have lucid or prophetic dreams, leave it near your bed or under it; if you want to improve your interpretation of oracle cards, keep it with you when dealing with divination; if you want to see visions in the bottle, shake it and look steadily but calmly at the liquid inside it.

A Witch's Bottle for Home Protection

This recipe is one of the most classic in the field of magic, being found in various traditions and cultures. Apparently, its origin is in old Europe, but it has spread so widely amongst Hoodoo practitioners that it can also be considered a heritage of this tradition. There is one very relevant point: this bottle can only be made by women! [109]

---

109. There are male versions of this recipe, but the fact is that the traditional formula is performed only by women.

Making it is very simple: Find a dark glass bottle with a lid. Inside it, put all sorts of sharp and piercing objects: razor blades, box cutters, needles, pins. Once this is done, you must complete it with your own urine, preferably during your menstrual period. Then, close the bottle and place it behind the house's front door or near it, preferably well hidden.

Magic Cookery

There are hundreds of magical recipes in Hoodoo, a tradition built from what you have on hand at home and—why not?—in the kitchen. This magic is done exactly like Violet Devereaux cooked her gumbo in the movie *The Skeleton Key*: cooking, but with intention! If you haven't seen the movie *The Skeleton Key*, then do, because it is all about Hoodoo! After that, enjoy our recipes!

Prosperity Meatballs

Meatballs are a classic recipe that can easily become a spell for prosperity as well.

Ingredients
Ground beef
Breadcrumbs
1 egg (for fertility)
1 cup of milk (for nutrition)

1 chopped red onion (for good luck)

Salt (for protection)

Ground black pepper (for protection)

Basil (for money, success, and happiness)

Nutmeg (for prosperity)

Olive oil (to bless)

How To

The trick here is to mix the ingredients while saying aloud the magical power of each one. Focus on the magical qualities of each ingredient as if you were an old fairy-tale witch preparing a magic potion.

It is very simple to make the meatball dough: mix everything, leaving the milk for last in order to get a soft consistency, but with enough firmness to roll into balls. (The size of the balls is up to you.) You can fry your meatballs in hot oil or cook them in a good tomato sauce.

Rose Sugar for Love

This sugar can be used however you'd like. It goes well in various sweets or even to sweeten juices, tea, and coffee. The recipe is extremely simple: In a mortar, pile sugar with rose petals. While you crush the sugar and roses, let yourself be filled with the purest feeling of love you can muster. (If you are in a bad mood, sad, or irritated, leave this recipe for another day!)

This mixture should rest for a week, covered with a thin layer of ordinary sugar. After that, just sift it and use your magic sugar to draw sighs from loving hearts and smiles of sympathy from your friends.

Reconciliation Pesto Sauce

For couples fighting, this recipe is a hit or miss!

Ingredients

Basil (for love and harmony in the family)

Parsley (for love)

Almonds (for love)

Olive oil (to bless)

Balsamic vinegar (to sweeten the sourness)

Parmesan cheese (to nourish the relationship)

Salt (for protection)

How To

First, recite Psalm 45 with your hands held over the olive oil. Mix the ingredients using a pestle or a food processor (in the case of the latter, the flavor will be more intense). Measure the basil, parsley, and salt to your taste. The almonds and parmesan will help to form the dough. The balsamic vinegar and olive oil should be added gradually; they will give the sauce a fluid texture. The mixture can be served with the pasta of your choice. But remember: state the magical properties of each ingredient as you add them to the recipe, and repeat your intention out loud as you prepare the dish.

Saint Expeditus's Cake to Achieve Grace

Make a novena to Saint Expeditus, asking him for what you need and promising him this cake if your request is granted. The saint has a weakness for this cake and will surely grant your wish quickly!

Ingredients

2 cups butter (to soften the paths)

4 cups wheat flour

2 cups sugar (to sweeten your life)

10 eggs (for spiritual cleansing)

1 teaspoon nutmeg (for prosperity)

1 teaspoon lemon juice (to ward off bad luck)

How To

Mix the butter and sugar until you get a soft, lump-free dough. Add the eggs one by one; only add the next egg after the previous egg has blended perfectly into the dough. Add the flour and nutmeg. Finally, add the lemon juice and beat very well. On a wide baking sheet, bake in an oven preheated to 300–325 degrees for eighty to ninety minutes.

Offer the cake in gratitude to Saint Expeditus, but be sure to taste it so that you benefit from its magic. And it doesn't hurt to remember: just like with other recipes, the magic happens during preparation. Therefore, follow the same guidelines, shared previously, when it comes to stating intention.

Good Luck Punch

This simple recipe offers good luck to whoever drinks it.

Ingredients

1 bottle of cider (for luck in love)

1 bottle of cranberry juice (to ward off enemies and break curses)

5 cinnamon sticks (for luck with money)

2 drops of vanilla essence (for luck in love)

How To

Let the cinnamon sit in the cider for half an hour. Remove it, then add the cranberry juice and vanilla essence. Let the drink rest in the refrigerator for one night. When serving, you can add red wine to taste.

CONCLUSION

We are reaching the end of our journey into the mysteries of Vodou, Voodoo, and Hoodoo. As a way of thanking you for your company so far, we have prepared an exclusive e-book with several other magical recipes. To access it, visit the website www.arolecultural.com.br /ebook/hoodoo-spells and register using the code MY-LLEWELLYN-VODOU-BOOK. You will then be able to access even more everyday Hoodoo spells free of charge!

BIBLIOGRAPHY

Alvarado, Denise. "The Superposition of Dr. Jean: A Handwriting Investigation." *Dr. John Montanee: A Grimoire*, edited by Dr. Louie Martinié, 160–72. Cincinnati, OH: Black Moon Publishing, 2019.

———. *The Voodoo Hoodoo Spellbook*. San Francisco: Weiser Books, 2011.

Anonymous. Review of *The Voodoo Queen*, by Robert Tallant. *Kirkus Reviews* (February 1955). https://www.kirkusreviews.com/book-reviews/a/robert-tallant-7/the-voodoo-queen.

Assis, Diego. "Cientista defende verdades por trás do mito dos zumbis." *Globo*, January 28, 2010. https://g1.globo.com/Noticias/PopArte/0,,MUL1466802-7084,00-CIENTISTA+DEFENDE+VERDADES+POR+TRAS+DO+MITO+DOS+ZUMBIS.html.

Beaubrun, Mimerose P. *Nan Dòmi: An Initiate's Journey into Haitian Vodou*. Translated by D. J. Walker. San Francisco: City Lights Books, 2013.

Bird, Stephanie Rose. *365 Days of Hoodoo: Daily Rootwork, Mojo & Conjuration*. Woodbury, MN: Llewellyn Publications, 2018.

Casas, Starr. *Old Style Conjure: Hoodoo, Rootwork & Folk Magic*. Newburyport, MA: Weiser Books, 2017.

———. *The Conjure Workbook, Volume 1: Working the Root*. Los Angeles: Pendraig Publishing, 2013.

Chireau, Yvonne, and Mambo Vye Zo Komande LaMenfo. "Esoteric Writing of Vodou: Grimoires, Sigils, and the Houngan's Notebook." *Esotericism in African American Religious Experience: There Is a Mystery*, edited by Stephen C. Finley, Margarita Simon Guillory, and Hugh R. Page Jr., 21–36. Leiden, Netherlands: Brill, 2014.

Corfield, Samantha, and Matthew Corfield. "The Priyè Ginen." DocPlayer. Accessed June 13, 2023. https://docplayer.net/41272583-The-priye-ginen-the-african-prayer.html.

Davis, Wade. *A Serpente E O Arco Iris: Zumbis Vodu Magia Negra*. São Paulo, Brazil: Zahar, 1986.

Deren, Maya. *Divine Horsemen: The Living Gods of Haiti*. Kingston, NY: McPherson & Company, 1998.

Fandrich, Ina Johanna. *The Mysterious Voodoo Queen, Marie Laveaux: A Study of Powerful Female Leadership in Nineteenth-Century New Orleans*. New York: Routledge, 2005.

Filan, Kenaz. *The Haitian Vodou Handbook: Protocols for Riding with the Lwa*. Rochester, VT: Destiny Books, 2006.

———. *The New Orleans Voodoo Handbook*. Rochester, VT: Destiny Books, 2011.

Frisvold, Nicholaj de Mattos. *A Arte dos Indomados*. São Paulo, Brazil: Penumbra Livros, 2011.

Galembo, Phyllis. *Vodou: Visions and Voices of Haiti*. Berkeley, CA: Ten Speed Press, 2005.

Gordon, Leah. *The Book of Vodou: Charms and Rituals to Empower Your Life*. Hauppauge, NY: B. E. S. Publishing, 2000.

"History of Lafayette Square." Lafayette Square Conservancy. Accessed November 30, 2023. https://lafayette-square.org/about-lsc/history.

Horne, Rebecca. "Picturing the Invisible: Seance." Lens Culture. Accessed June 13, 2023. https://www.lensculture.com/articles/shannon-taggart-picturing-the-invisible-seance.

Katherine, Miss. *Psalms & Hoodoo*. Self-published, 2018.

Ladies Auxiliary of Missionary Independent Spiritual Church. *Hoodoo Food!: The Best of the Conjure Cook-Off and Rootwork Recipe Round-Up. Missionary Independent Spiritual Church*. Edited by Sister Robin Petersen. Self-published, 2014.

Lady Hannah. "The History of Candle Colour in Hoodoo." Hoodoo Witch, April 3, 2022. https://hoodoo witch.net/how-to-use-coloured-candles-in-hoodoo/.

Lago, Jorge, Laura P. Rodríguez, Lucía Blanco, Juan Manuel Vieites, and Ana G. Cabado. "Tetrodotoxin, an Extremely Potent Marine Neurotoxin: Distribution, Toxicity, Origin, and Therapeutical Uses." *Marine Drugs* 13, no. 10 (2015): 6384–406. https://doi.org/10.3390/md13106384.

LaMenfo, Mambo Vye Zo Komande. *Serving the Spirits: The Religion of Haitian Vodou*. Self-published, 2011.

Laurence. L. W. de. *The Great Book of Magical Art, Hindu Magic, and East Indian Occultism*. London: Forgotten Books, 2018.

Little, Myles. "Basement Vodou: Haitian Spirituality in Brooklyn." *TIME*, September 25, 2012. https://time.com/3791786/vodou.

Long, Carolyn Morrow. "Marie Laveau Timeline." World Religions and Spirituality Project, October 27, 2017. https://wrldrels.org/2017/10/27/marie-laveau.

———. *A New Orleans Voudou Priestess: The Legend and Reality of Marie Laveau*. Gainesville: University Press of Florida, 2006.

———. *Spiritual Merchants: Religion, Magic & Commerce*. Knoxville: University of Tennessee Press, 2001.

Martinié, Louie. *Dr. John Montanee: A Grimoire*. Cincinnati, OH: Black Moon Publishing, 2019.

Métraux, Alfred. *Voodoo in Haiti*. Translated by Hugo Charteris. New York: Pantheon, 1989.

Millett, Deacon. *Hoodoo Honey and Sugar Spells: Sweet Love Magic in the Conjure Tradition*. Forestville, CA: Lucky Mojo Curio Company, 2013.

Moise, Hoodoo Sen. *Working Conjure: A Guide to Hoodoo Folk Magic*. Newburyport, MA: Weiser Books, 2018.

Neves, Márcia Cristina A. *Do Vodu à Macumba*. São Paulo, Brazil: Tríade Editorial, 1991.

Office of International Religious Freedom. "2021 Report on International Religious Freedom: Benin." US Department of State, June 2, 2022. https://www.state .gov/reports/2021-report-on-international-religious -freedom/benin.

"Pessoas Especiais: Marie Laveau." *O Arquivo* (The Archive), blog. Accessed December 7, 2023. https:// www.oarquivo.com.br/extraordinario/pessoas -especiais/4091-marie-laveau.html.

Potter, Eliza. *A Hairdresser's Experience in High Life*. Edited by Xiomara Santamarina. Chapel Hill: The University of North Carolina Press, 2009.

Quiareli, Diogo. "A história de Papa Legba, uma figura de vodu vista como a mais diabólica." Fatos Desconhecidos, October 23, 2018. https://www.fatosdes conhecidos.com.br/historia-de-papa-legba-uma -figura-de-vodu-vista-como-mais-diabolica.

Rigaud, Milo. *Secrets of Voodoo*. Translated by Robert B. Cross. San Francisco: City Lights Publishers, 2001.

———, ed. *Ve-Ve Diagrammes Rituels du Voudou: Ritual Voodoo Diagrams: Blasones de los Vodu*. Trilingual ed. New York: French & European Publications, 1992.

Selig, Godfrey. *The Secrets of the Psalms: The Key to Answered Prayers from the King James Bible*. Self-published, 2014.

Selwanga, Frater. "O Asson no Vodou." *OTOA LCN Brasil* (blog), August 19, 2020. https://www.otoa-lcn -brasil.com.br/post/o-asson-no-vodou.

Tallant, Robert. *Voodoo in New Orleans*. Gretna, NE: Pelican Publishing Company, 1983.

———. *The Voodoo Queen*. Gretna, NE: Pelican Publishing Company, 2003.

Tann, Mambo Chita. *Haitian Vodou: An Introduction to Haiti's Indigenous Spiritual Tradition.* Woodbury, MN: Llewellyn Publications, 2012.

Toledano, Roulhac. *The National Trust Guide to New Orleans: The Definitive Guide to Architectural and Cultural Treasures.* New York: John Wiley & Sons, 1996.

Vameri, Frater. "A Sereia das Antilhas." *OTOA LCN Brasil* (blog), November 12, 2019. https://www.otoa-lcn -brasil.com.br/post/a-sereia-das-antilhas.

———. "Barão Samedi: um Lwa a rigor (mortis)." *OTOA LCN Brasil* (blog), November 30, 2019. https://www.otoa-lcn-brasil.com.br/post/bar %C3%A3o-samedi-um-Lwa-a-rigor-mortis.

———. "Erzulie Freda: feminilidade e perfeição no Vodou." *OTOA LCN Brasil* (blog), November 19, 2019. https://www.otoa-lcn-brasil.com.br/post /erzulie-freda-feminilidade-e-perfei%C3%A7 %C3%A3o-no-vodou.

———. "Gran Bwa: a árvore dos mundos." *OTOA LCN Brasil* (blog), December 10, 2019. https://www.otoa -lcn-brasil.com.br/post/gran-bwa-a-%C3%A1rvore -dos-mundos.

———. "Loko e Ayizan." *OTOA LCN Brasil* (blog), August 5, 2020. https://www.otoa-lcn-brasil.com .br/post/loko-e-ayizan.

———. "Manman Brijit - a dona do cemitério." *OTOA LCN Brasil* (blog), August 12, 2020. https://www.otoa-lcn-brasil.com.br/post/manman-brijit-a-dona-do-cemit%C3%A9rio.

———. "Os Gêmeos No Vodou." *OTOA LCN Brasil* (blog), September 23, 2020. https://www.otoa-lcn-brasil.com.br/post/os-g%C3%AAmeos-no-vodou.

———. "Papa Legba: Abrindo os Portões." *Otoa Lcn Brasil* (blog), January 14, 2020. https://www.otoa-lcn-brasil.com.br/post/papa-legba-abrindo-os-port%C3%B5es.

———. "Templo e ferramentas do Vodou." *OTOA LCN Brasil* (blog), June 24, 2020. https://www.otoa-lcn-brasil.com.br/post/templo-e-ferramentas-do-vodou.

———. "Um pouco sobre Ogou." *OTOA LCN Brasil* (blog), October 22, 2019. https://www.otoa-lcn-brasil.com.br/post/um-pouco-sobre-ogou.

Vilsaint, Féquière, and Maude Heurtelou. *Diksyonè Kreyòl Vilsen.* 3rd ed. Temple Terrace, FL: Educa Vision. https://ufdc.ufl.edu/AA00010738/00001.

"Vodou, Serving the Spirits." The Pluralism Project. Accessed November 27, 2023. https://pluralism.org/vodou-serving-the-spirits.

Ward, Martha. *Voodoo Queen: The Spirited Lives of Marie Laveau.* Jackson: University Press of Mississippi, 2004.

yronwode, catherine. *Hoodoo Herb and Root Magic: A Materia Magica of African-American Conjure.* Forestville, CA: Lucky Mojo Curio Company, 2002.

———. *Paper in My Shoe: Name Papers, Petition Papers, and Prayer Papers in Hoodoo, Rootwork, and Conjure.* Forestville, CA: Lucky Mojo Curio Company, 2015.

yronwode, catherine, and Lara Rivera. *Bottle Up and Go!: The Magic of Hoodoo Container Spells in Boxes, Jars, Bags, Bowls, and Buckets.* Forestville, CA: Lucky Mojo Curio Company, 2020.

To Write to the Authors

If you wish to contact the authors or would like more information about this book, please write to the authors in care of Llewellyn Worldwide Ltd. and we will forward your request. Both the authors and publisher appreciate hearing from you and learning of your enjoyment of this book and how it has helped you. Llewellyn Worldwide Ltd. cannot guarantee that every letter written to the authors can be answered, but all will be forwarded. Please write to:

Sebastien de la Croix
Diamantino Fernandes Trindade
℅ Llewellyn Worldwide
2143 Wooddale Drive
Woodbury, MN 55125-2989

Please enclose a self-addressed stamped envelope for reply,
or $1.00 to cover costs. If outside the U.S.A., enclose
an international postal reply coupon.

Many of Llewellyn's authors have websites with additional information and resources. For more information, please visit our website at http://www.llewellyn.com.